Great Parents,
Lousy Lovers

GREAT
PARENTS

Lousy
Lovers

Discover how to enjoy life with
your spouse while raising your kids

DR. GARY SMALLEY
& TED CUNNINGHAM

TYNDALE HOUSE PUBLISHERS, INC., CAROL STREAM, ILLINOIS

Visit Tyndale's exciting Web site at www.tyndale.com.

TYNDALE and Tyndale's quill logo are registered trademarks of Tyndale House Publishers, Inc.

Great Parents, Lousy Lovers: Discover How to Enjoy Life with Your Spouse While Raising Your Kids

Copyright © 2010 by Gary Smalley and Ted Cunningham. All rights reserved.

Cover font love-ya-like-a-sister copyright © by Kimberly Geswein. All rights reserved.

Author photo of Gary Smalley copyright © by Jim Lersch. All rights reserved.

Author photo of Ted Cunningham copyright © 2009 by Renee Bergman. All rights reserved.

Designed by Jennifer Ghionzoli

Produced in association with Roger Gibson, Branson, Missouri.

All Scripture quotations, unless otherwise indicated, are taken from the Holy Bible, *New International Version,*® *NIV.*® Copyright © 1973, 1978, 1984 by Biblica, Inc.™ Used by permission of Zondervan. All rights reserved worldwide. www.zondervan.com.

Scripture quotations marked NLT are taken from the *Holy Bible*, New Living Translation, copyright © 1996, 2004, 2007 by Tyndale House Foundation. Used by permission of Tyndale House Publishers, Inc., Carol Stream, Illinois 60188. All rights reserved.

Scripture quotations marked ASV are taken from *The Holy Bible*, American Standard Version.

Scripture quotations marked NKJV are taken from the New King James Version.® Copyright © 1982 by Thomas Nelson, Inc. Used by permission. All rights reserved. *NKJV* is a trademark of Thomas Nelson, Inc.

Scripture quotations marked NASB are taken from the New American Standard Bible,® copyright © 1960, 1962, 1963, 1968, 1971, 1972, 1973, 1975, 1977, 1995 by The Lockman Foundation. Used by permission.

Library of Congress Cataloging-in-Publication Data

Smalley, Gary.
   Great parents, lousy lovers : discover how to enjoy life with your spouse while raising your kids / Gary Smalley and Ted Cunningham.
      p. cm.
   Includes bibliographical references.
   ISBN 978-1-4143-3588-9 (hc)
   1. Spouses—Religious life.   2. Parents—Religious life.   3. Marriage—Religious aspects—Christianity.   4. Parenting—Religious aspects—Christianity.   I. Cunningham, Ted.   II. Title.
   BV4596.M3S62 2010
   248.8'45—dc22   2010020834

Printed in the United States of America

16   15   14   13   12   11   10
7   6   5   4   3   2   1

We dedicate this book to the fantastic staff and elders at
Woodland Hills Family Church in Branson, Missouri.
Ted Burden, Denise Bevins, Stephanie Watson,
Brenda Pannell, Angela Jennings, Amy Cunningham,
Pam Strayer, John Meyer, Jim Sedlacek, Bill Rogers,
Mike Gattis, Doug Hayter, and Doug Goodwin
serve marriages and families in our church and community
with excellence. We love and appreciate each one of you.

Contents

Acknowledgments

Thank you to Amy Cunningham and Norma Smalley for sharing your stories for this project. We love you both very much.

Roger Gibson has believed in this project since we first mentioned the title to him. He got it immediately and quickly became a passionate advocate for getting the message out there. Thanks, Rog!

The entire team at Tyndale rocks! Thank you, Ron Beers and Jon Farrar, for believing in our message. Stephanie Voiland, you were a joy and pleasure to work with. Stephanie Krzywonos, thank you for blessing our message and getting everyone on board. Thanks also to Lisa Jackson, Erin Marshall, Erin Gwynne, Jennifer Ghionzoli, Vicky Lynch, April Kimura-Anderson, Keith Johnson, and Amanda Reckinger.

Denise Bevins, Sue Parks, Jeff Smethers, and Pam Strayer take care of so many details in our ministries from day to day. It does not go unnoticed, and we are so grateful.

CHAPTER 1

GENERATION OBSERVATION

You might be a Great Parent, Lousy Lover if you grew up in the '80s, rolled up your pants, poufed your bangs, drove a Camaro, or have more than two Bryan Adams songs memorized.

GARY... I love observation. Norma and I are that couple at the restaurant watching other families. Part of our regular entertainment is making up stories about what we observe. We often catch ourselves laughing, shaking our heads, or even tearing up as we think about the countless stories unfolding in families around us. We see the excitement of families as they eat out in Branson, Missouri, enjoying the first day of their vacation. We can even identify the families that are eating a quick bite after exhausting themselves at one of our theme parks on the last day of their vacation. I can spot a loving and caring dad from a mile away. I can also tell when he's distant and angry. I can see the spirit of a woman when it is crushed. My wife, Norma, is an expert at sniffing out the child who has Mom and Dad wrapped around his or her little finger. We're not judgmental; we're just old, and we eat out a lot. It gives us plenty of time to observe.

I am my own scientific study of one. Over the years, I have studied research comparing the biological brain patterns in preschoolers and how they translate into the gender differences. Through our work with thousands of couples at the Smalley Relationship Center, we have learned the best practices for working with crisis couples. I have personally interviewed over sixty thousand women to discover what leads to deep and lasting intimacy. Now at it for more than forty years, I am convinced that my own personal scientific study has impacted me the most. My entire ministry has been built on making mistakes in my marriage and family, repairing the relationships, and passing on what I have learned. I have even been accused of messing up on purpose so I would have something to write about. Ha! I wish I were nearing perfection to the point I had to fake mistakes. Wouldn't that be something?

Alive for seventy years, I have observed a lot. Moses says we get seventy years, eighty if we're strong, but I'm pushing for ninety. Married for forty-five of those years, I have now observed four generations within my own family. First I observed my parents and how they raised me. My second observation included everything Norma and I did with our children, most of which was opposite of my parents. My third observation could possibly be my favorite: my kids' correcting everything Norma and I did wrong with them. It hurts sometimes, but it is hilarious more often than not. They have also picked up and passed along our good habits. And my last observation (which is in its very early stages) is of my grandkids and how they are experiencing life reacting to their moms and dads. Lord knows, I love being the patriarch.

Every generation has unique characteristics. I have been particularly interested in the differences of each generation when it comes to marriage and parenting. The parents of today view the world and their role in it entirely differently than Norma and I. It hasn't been that long, but I don't remember ever having guilt as part of our parenting style. Sure there were times when I returned home from a speaking trip and felt guilty for being away. Or the times when I corrected or disciplined the kids only to learn that I was the one who was wrong. Guilt was rare. We did the best we could with the skills we had. Looking back, there are many, many things I would do differently. That's the beauty of hindsight. But for the most part, I have few regrets.

Not so with today's parents. They live for each and every moment as though they are going to miss something. Birthday parties seem more extravagant than ever. Disney is an annual goal, rather than a lifetime achievement. Kids get their own rooms; heaven forbid they share one. They have their first car at three, albeit a Barbie Jeep or John Deere Gator. Every day is a special day at school. Wear something green day. Funky hair day. Silly socks day. Awards assembly day. Pajama party day. You get the gist. When I was a kid, we were lucky to get an annual field trip to the library. Oh no! Did I just give the "When I was a kid" line? Am I coming across like a grumpy old man? I promise I'm not grumpy. But this is fun. Let's keep going.

Parents today are rushing their kids from karate to dance while doing homework in the car and grabbing a bite at a drive-through. We sign our kids up for everything special. Forget about making costumes for Halloween; Target and Walmart have the latest and greatest in Hannah Montana and superhero attire. "Seize the day" has turned into "soak up everything out there, and squeeze every last drop of life out of the day." We give all of our time and energy to the kids and very little to the marriage. Every hour a parent is not working or sleeping is given with a big bow on top to the kids. To not do so makes you a bad parent.

My young friend Jon Jenkins in Branson put it best when he said, "Gary, my dad loved me very much. I have never questioned that. He worked hard, and I don't ever remember him coming home and spending hours playing with me and my brother. At best we would get a quick game of catch or a pickup basketball game, but then he was on to mow the lawn, change the oil in the car, grill dinner for Mom, or fix little things around the house. When he moved on to household chores, I don't ever remember feeling like he didn't love me. Why do I feel so guilty if I need to get something done around the house? Heather believes that we need to spend way more time with our kids than our parents could or would spend with us."

Observation #1—My Parents

My parents' generation, the Builders, was born between 1922 and 1943. They lived through the Great Depression and World War II. They were taught to value hard work, law and order, and respect for authority. Their generation was built on surviving. They faced many hardships and were grateful if there was food on the table every night.

The Builder generation is also called the "Greatest Generation." This is the generation of sacrifice. This generation not only saved the world for us; they also built our country for us through sacrifice and hard work. They were willing to do whatever it took to get the job done. They are people of duty, loyalty, and honor. Your grandparents probably had the same job or profession for their entire working career. Once these people took a job, they didn't quit it, and they outlasted many bosses.

My dad worked, and my mom stayed home. Mom worked outside of the home only if it was absolutely necessary to provide for the family. Because they survived the Great Depression, survival was their first priority around the home, not comfort or fun. Because commitment was such a high value, they would settle for a mediocre marriage so long as they never divorced. They stayed married because divorce would bring undue hardship upon the family, and family was their highest priority. However, children and family were not synonymous. There was a strong family structure, and Dad was very much in charge. The Builders coined the phrase

"Wait until your father gets home." In other words, "Daddy's gonna give it to ya if you don't shape up." Kid-centered homes were rare in my parents' generation.

I had a very angry father who lived with the "Kids should be seen and not heard" motto. My dad and I did not spend a lot of time together. I can remember his occasional outbursts around the dinner table followed by an immediate departure. His exit was a relief to the entire family. We could get on with the meal in peace.

Dad was the provider. Mom was the caregiver. That would change with me. I was going to be a provider and a caregiver. I would do everything with my kids that Dad never did with me.

Observation #2—My Generation

The Boomers were born between 1943 and 1960. I was actually born in 1940, but everything in my being screams Boomer. Defining events for the Boomers include television, the civil rights movement, and prosperity. We value health and wellness, personal growth, and civic involvement.

While my parents' generation considered themselves lucky because they survived the Depression and a world war, the Boomer generation feels more stress than luck. Many Builders lost their jobs and were pushed out with early retirement because there were so many Boomers who drove them out and took the management positions. Boomers are the CEOs, CFOs, COOs, and managers right now.

Boomers live with the buy-now-pay-later mentality, and they live to work. They view themselves as important when they are successful. This success-driven mind-set set the pace for their parenting as well.

My generation was the first set of parents to create the "My child is an honor roll student" bumper stickers. Your grandparents did not use such stickers. We enrolled our kids in gifted reading programs and honors classes. We made our children study hard for those ACT and SAT tests so they could get into good schools and eventually find good jobs. Health plans, 401(k)s, and job security are high values.

I grew up in a very poor home with a very angry father. Most of my parenting skills were birthed from an attitude that said, "I'm going to do everything the opposite way my dad did it." I heard all the time growing up, "I didn't have it; you don't need it." I in turn told my children, "I didn't get it, so I'm going to make sure you do." Since God blessed me with resources to do so, I gave my kids everything. I wanted to make sure my kids had everything I didn't. I raised three Buster children.

Observation #3—My Kids

My kids' generation, the Busters, was born between 1960 and 1980. Watergate, Michael Jackson, and the fall of the Berlin Wall were defining moments for this generation. They value diversity, global thinking, and pragmatism.

My kids rolled up their pant legs, spiked their bangs,

played Trivial Pursuit, and watched Harrison Ford play Indiana Jones in all the sequels.

My parents were emotionally disconnected from me, and I never heard my dad say, "I love you." The real question for me was "How many times a day will my kids hear 'I love you' from me?" Your parents decided to fix the emotional disconnection but made the mistake of connecting with you financially rather than emotionally. Your parents thought, *We are going to pay for your college. Don't even worry about getting a job to buy books; we're going to pay for your books, too. You don't need to work in the off-season of college; I want you to relax the three months of summer and the month at Christmas and the week at Easter and the week at Thanksgiving.* That's why, when a Buster comes in to interview with a Boomer, one of the first three questions they ask is "How much time off do I get?" Boomers view Busters as lazy. Busters just consider themselves more relaxed; a little more laid back. They have decided not to be as stressed out as the Boomer generation.

Compared to previous generations, this pampered upbringing has led to entitlement. As a whole, Busters tend to want in three years what their parents have spent thirty years accumulating. I saw this in my own family. My children wanted in their twenties the success I had in my forties and fifties. When they didn't achieve it, they felt let down. Boomers call hard-earned accomplishment paying your dues and earning your stripes. Those with an entitled mind-set not only want a quick payoff, but believe for some reason that they deserve it. Later in the book we will look at how this sense of entitlement creeps into parenting and can put unrealistic expectations on grandparents.

The Busters see life as full of options. If this job doesn't work out in a couple of months, they'll find another one. They'll have more jobs by the time they turn thirty than my generation ever dreamed of having in a lifetime.

So far we have looked at the differences in my generation and my kids' generation. Now let's look at the one glaring similarity. Know what it is? We have in common the kid-centered home. We both treat our kids like gold. We are going to connect with them in every way possible. In addition to money, Busters connect with more time. They'll even disconnect from, or divorce, their spouses if they think it will be better for the kids. Every waking minute is geared around the kids. To invest in a hobby or another group of friends is to be selfish, and it leads to poor parenting. In many ways this is smothering their Bridger children.

Observation #4—My Grandchildren

Unlike any other generation in history, the Bridgers get massive amounts of attention from the preceding two generations. Grandma and Grandpa pick up the slack where Mom and Dad leave off or when they are unavailable. Think about how far we have come. The other day my grandson texted me from school, asking me to grab him some Sonic and then pick him up from school. When I was a kid . . . Nope, I'm not even going there.

Bridgers were born after 1980. Defining events include school violence, multiculturalism, reality TV, and terrorism. They value civic duty, achievement, and diversity.

The Bridgers are also referred to as millennials or mosaics. They are also called the iPod generation. This generation is still defining themselves, and they want to be approached on their own terms. Really? Does that surprise you? They've been raised to set the rules. They want to set the playing field. They are still coming to understand who they are and what they are going to be. To be honest with you, generational studies and researchers are saying the Builders and Boomers have more hope for the Bridgers than for the Busters.

Now you may have read through my four observations about the generations and thought, *That's not me or my parents at all.* There are always exceptions, but the characteristics bleed over into our culture. While your parents may have raised you very differently from your friends, our parenting styles are influenced by the culture we live in. We see what other parents are doing, and we all can feel the pressure to conform.

Our church regularly hosts playgroups for moms with young children. As the kids play, the moms spend their time discussing best practices. They exchange information on formula, deals on clothes, and whether or not their kids will make the cutoff for kindergarten. Swapping stories is what we do as young parents, and it is not a bad thing at all. It takes a village. So while you may not have been raised in the stereotypical Boomer home, you may have friends who were, and they are influencing your parenting today.

Will you journey with me as we make some observations and discoveries together? Throughout this book I hope you have many "That is totally us" moments. We are all on this parenting journey together. I've asked my pastor and great friend, Ted Cunningham, to join me on this quest. This is my fourth book with Ted. He is a fantastic guy to work with, and I love how his brain works. We spend a lot of time together in life, and he constantly challenges me to stay fresh and on my "A" game. I'd feel a lot older than I actually am if I ever stopped hanging around guys like Ted. He is a great teacher and writer, and I know you will enjoy his observations as well.

Before we go on our discovery, I want you to get to know Ted a little better. He is a Buster who struggles to keep from becoming a Great Parent, Lousy Lover.

Add your voice to the GPLL message . . .

Connect with us at www.greatparentslousylovers.com and watch the video podcast for chapter 1.

Post your thoughts, comments, and stories on our Web site. Here are some questions from chapter 1 to get you started on your journey to a couple-centered home:

- What kind of home did you grow up in? Kid centered or couple centered?
- Which generation do you best relate to?

- What are some of the attributes of your generation's parenting styles?
- What about your parenting style is different from the cultural norms of your generation?
- Even though we are early in the journey together, can you identify some changes that you need to make in your home?

OBSERVATION DATE:

Sit down with your spouse—at home or away—for an "observation conversation." What do you each observe about the state of your individual hearts, your kids' hearts, and the heart of your family? What are signs of health in each? What are some areas of concern? Include a favorite snack, and share at least one memory that makes you smile.

CHAPTER 2

PRINCESS AND QUEEN

You might be a Great Parent, Lousy Lover if you feel like a cook, maid, or shuttle, and you run your home like a hotel.

TED... I'm only thirty-six years old, and Gary has already turned me into an observation freak. His friendship and mentoring have given me a lens beneath the surface of life. My family eats out with Gary and Norma a couple of times a month, and it still amazes me how they can laugh at my feeble attempts at parenting. Can I let you in on a little secret? My beloved coauthor will even egg on my kids to get a rise out of me. He will request the opposite behavior I desire just so he can "observe" my parenting skills. Love you, Gary.

I do not have the years of observation that Gary has. My learning these days comes from a lot of trial and error. Will Rogers once said, "There are three kinds of men. The one that learns by reading. The few who learn by observation. The rest of them have to pee on the electric fence for themselves."

In the fall of 2006, I had to make some serious changes at home. With a three-year-old and a one-year-old, Amy and I were losing the passion for each other. We were not fighting, but we made no time for each other. We were living in a vacuum of intimacy. We loved our kids, but they sure were sucking the life right out of our marriage. I longed for the times when Amy would simply walk into the room and take my breath away. I wanted her back in my arms. I dreamed, and yes, sometimes fantasized, about kissing her and loving on her the way we did before our kids were born. Truth be told, she felt the same way, but we didn't know what to do about the sad situation. I knew if changes were going to be made at home, I would need to not only initiate them but also lead and model them.

One morning during a devotional time I realized something that would change the pace of our home. In order to remove the vacuum of intimacy, Amy had to be established as the queen of our home. She had to be elevated in the eyes of the whole family. I would need to perform a coronation service and ensure two new rules at home. First, when the queen is talking, no one else speaks. She has the floor. We wait until she is done, then we may speak. Second, no one runs ahead of the queen. We follow her in everything we do. You will soon realize that once the husband begins treating his wife as the queen, she very quickly begins treating him as a king, which leads very quickly into a whole new level of intimacy in the marriage chamber!

It had been a cold winter in Branson, and without knowing it we had slipped into some bad habits. When we would pull into the parking lot of the grocery store or a restaurant, Amy and I would each grab a child. Amy took a little longer than me and would say, "You guys run on ahead." Since it was cold, that made sense. So I would dart into the building and wait inside for her and our son, Carson.

Well, as these two breakthrough rules took root, the first person I couldn't wait to share them with was my daughter, who was only three at the time. Shortly after arriving home that night, I scooped Corynn up and asked if we could talk. She responded with, "Sure, Daddy!"

"Corynn," I said, "I need to apologize to you and Mommy. I have not been setting a good example around here. As of tonight, I will be making changes. To start with, I need you to know that there is only one queen in this home and you are not her."

Corynn's face went blank. She didn't say a word and waited for me to continue. So I did. "Mommy is the queen, and that means that, when she talks, we do not. No one speaks when the queen is talking. She has the floor. Okay?"

"Okay," Corynn said, still looking a bit confused. But I could tell she was getting it.

"Second, no one runs ahead of the queen. What that means is you and I will no longer run ahead into stores or restaurants and wait for Mommy and Carson. Even if that means we freeze our patooties off, we are waiting for them. Okay?"

"Okay," she said as she skipped into the other room.

The conversation was over for now, and I would start practicing what I had just declared. The next day Amy and Corynn went on a mommy-daughter date. Corynn was acting reserved and not her usual, bubbly self. Amy asked her, "What's the matter, sweetie?"

"Daddy won't let me be the queen," Corynn blurted.

Deep down Amy was thrilled. As parents you've got to love when you think a conversation went in one ear and right out the other, only to learn later that they really did get it. When they got home from the date, Amy told me about the conversation. I was thrilled but knew I was not finished sharing with Corynn. My conversation was only half complete, so I went into the family room to find Corynn so we could finish our little talk about Mommy's "queen-ness."

"Corynn, Daddy needs to talk. Guess what?"

"What?" Corynn inquired, tilting her head.

"Remember yesterday when I told you that Mommy was the one and only queen in this home? I forgot to finish the story. Mommy may be my only queen, but you, Corynn Mae Cunningham, are my one and only *princess*." Her eyes lit up! There is not a person on the planet who knows more about Cinderella, Belle, Aurora, Ariel, Snow White, Jasmine, or Pocahontas than me! I've seen them all on video and live more than once. Oh, we love the princesses. This was a word picture Corynn got, and I could tell her heart was filling with joy.

"Corynn, God wants me to prepare you for your coronation. You will be a queen one day. One of the best ways you can learn to do that is by watching me take care of my queen, your mommy. That way you will know what to look for in a husband. You'll look for a husband who treats you like a queen."

When I come home from work, there is a series of questions that must be answered before our family evening begins.

As my children run to hug me, I yell out, "Who's the queen of this house?"

"Mommmmmmmy!" Corynn and Carson shout.

"Who's the princess?" I ask.

"I ammmmmmmmm!" Corynn screams with her hand raised.

"Who's the prince?"

"Meeeeeeeeeee!" Carson jumps in.

"Who is the king of this house?" I ask with even greater enthusiasm.

The answer is always the same: "JESUS!"

I'm still trying to find my place in the Cunningham family.

There's one more reason why I have a propensity to neglect my marriage. When I choose to push my marriage down on the list of priorities, it is usually at the end of a long, exhausting day. Time and energy are key ingredients to a great marriage. When I reach empty on my energy, emotional, and physical tanks, I try to convince myself that it is just for a season and that we'll reconnect later. As parents we are easily tempted to give our children everything they need at the expense of marriage. I don't want Amy to get the loose change of my spending.

I like to ask myself this question: *Ted, how do you view your son and daughter?* Words like *precious, beautiful,* and *gifts from God* come to mind. When they need something, I try to respond with all the energy required to meet that need. While it can be frustrating, tiresome, and difficult to meet my children's every need, I rarely question whether they deserve the care. So what's left for Amy? Often nothing. That leads me to another important question: "How do I value my wife?" The same words and more come to mind. Precious. Beautiful. Gift from God. Selfless. Lover. Best Friend. Woman of God.

Great parent and great lover is my goal. I believe that great parenting is the overflow of a great marriage. I am husband, father, pastor, son, friend, author, and handyman with the same twenty-four hours in a day as every other human on the planet. Guarding and growing my marriage during these long days is a choice I get to make every morning. Most parents I meet who still have children at home are tired, very tired. If they are not getting ready to go someplace, they are just coming back. Coming or going seems to be the pattern for most parents today. The pace of our parenting quickly outruns the pace of our marriage, and each spouse feels neglected or forgotten. It's in these emotions that evil thoughts can begin to take root.

A friend of mine once told me his grandmother always

said, "Remember, Mikey, when you grow up and get married, you better court your gal every day, or someone else will!" That is wise advice from a woman born in 1898. Parenting is not for the weak. Those who are parenting while still growing a great marriage are pretty much at the hero level for me. It takes hard work, but the payoff is huge.

During the first couple of years as a brand-new dad, I would get frustrated when people would tell me to enjoy those early years because they go by so fast. I'd smile, but inside I was thinking, *Yadda-yadda-yadda*. Those kind words of advice were tough to hear after the eighth wet and second poopy diaper of the day or after a major temper tantrum in a mall. Then it started happening regularly. People would walk by me at a restaurant or a store and say, "Your kids are so cute. You better soak up every moment because it will be over before you know it." I was thinking, *We still have bath time tonight, which can be a living nightmare, plus I know there's the chance of one final poopy diaper, and with all that, I am still hoping Amy is in the mood for a little marital bliss!*

One night my wife and I were sharing dinner with a pastor and his wife, and as they asked about our children, the pastor's wife said something I will never forget: "It bothered me so bad when people would tell me to soak up every moment because they go so fast." Amy and I became immediate kindred spirits with her. She got it! *This woman is brilliant*, I thought to myself. She validated the sleep deprivation we were experiencing, and we knew we were not alone on this journey. She went on to say, "Keep this in mind: The days go slow, but the years go fast." That I got! That finally made sense. The days were robbing us of sleep. The days were exhausting. The days required meeting endless demands and at times a lot of whining, mostly mine. Can you say, "Grow up, Ted!"

We no longer have preschoolers at home. That stage of life is over for us. And to tell you the truth, I miss it. I miss Carson stumbling over his first words and learning how to adjust his feet so he doesn't trip and fall. I miss Corynn asking for Eskimo kisses, her sweet, little-girl voice pleading, "Daddy, kiss my nose, kiss my lips." Those bedtime rituals are gone forever. Now I watch as the years of their lives are flying by, while the days are still going by so slowly for Amy and me. If I'm not careful, my marriage can slip away as quickly as my children do. The day is coming when my children will be raised and gone with families of their own. I want them to look back toward home and see their mom and dad still crazy in love.

Add your voice to the GPLL message . . .

Connect with us at www.greatparentslousylovers.com and watch the video podcast for chapter 2.

Post your thoughts, comments, and stories on our Web site. Here are some questions from chapter 2 to get you started on your journey to a couple-centered home:

- Is Mom the "queen" of your home?
- Does your daughter show signs of wanting to be the "queen"? Point to a few of the signs.
- Is your son the "king"? Point to a few of the signs.

- Dad, what could you do better in establishing your wife as the "queen"?
- Mom, what steps could you take to honor Dad and teach that to your royal subjects?

CORONATION DATE:

Honor each other with the royal treatment. What does your spouse enjoy most? A back rub? Uninterrupted listening? A favorite movie? A favorite meal? Your answer to that question determines what you do on your date.

Note: This date is actually two in one since each of you gets a turn receiving the royal treatment.

CHAPTER 3

PREPARING FOR CHANGE

You might be a Great Parent, Lousy Lover if you consider an appetizer the free applesauce that comes with a kid's meal.

TED… "I don't plan on anything changing," I declared to the group. Amy and I had just found out we were expecting. We were full of excitement, but long on ignorance. It doesn't help to make stupid statements like that when you are in a small group with three marriage and family therapists.

"What do you mean nothing will change?" the group asked collectively.

"The church is young and growing, and we will keep right on track," I assured everyone.

The snickering began. Three of the five couples had multiple children. They knew what was coming, and now they had to share with me a dose of reality.

"Ted, I see this a lot in couples. They get married, and one or both want to maintain aspects of single life. They continue to have regular nights out with the boys multiple times a week, games and practices with the team, and workouts alone. Then they have kids. I know of one mom who clubs several nights a week with her two-year-old at home," one member of the group shared.

"Yeah, I ain't doing any of that. Heck, I never did that when I was single," I self-righteously declared.

He continued, "Okay, for you it is meetings, visits, and studying, but it is the same idea. You will need to say no to people like you haven't in the past."

I armed myself and was ready for a fight. Serving the church was our life. We took busloads of kids to camp every summer, spending countless nights in cabins with dozens of elementary students. You'd think that would prepare a guy for parenting. But I was clueless. And at camp I fell asleep every night with the hope of my own bed a few days away.

Long nights preparing for holiday performances or vacation Bible school were routine for us. Dinners out with members of the church came to be expected. Staff outings became a way of life, and we loved every minute of it.

Our small group formed around the same time we started Woodland Hills Church. Getting a church off the ground required a ton of time and two tons of energy. Our workweek averaged sixty to eighty hours. We never complained about the work, though, because it was our passion. It was an overflow of our lives and consumed our conversations, trips to the store, and evening laptop time. There was always something to do. And since we were the only two staff members of a five-hundred-member church, it was on us to "git'r'done." My plan was to buy a BabyBjörn, strap the child on, and away we go. From clueless to brainless!

"Nothing is going to change once the baby is born," I declared with the same authority as the president delivering the State of the Union.

While I was defending my pastorate, I had no idea what my words were doing to my wife. She sat there in silence. Who would have thought she was on the side of the Stoevers, Houstons, and Smalleys? My words were not intended to hurt; they were simply my attempt to assure everyone that we would continue leading the church with all of our time and energy. I had no idea how badly they would hurt Amy. The fallout from those ill-chosen words would change our marriage forever. More importantly, it changed me forever. It was the beginning of me getting my brains back and starting to get a clue.

Amy heard them completely differently, and they rocked her world. She heard, "We are still going to work long hours each week. We will still go out to dinner regularly with friends. We will put in long nights at church. Don't expect our lives or schedules to be any different." Nothing could have been further from the reality that would soon engulf our lives.

Woman's intuition is like Superman's X-ray vision into the heart. Amy saw my heart when I said nothing would change. She knew I was not prepared for reality. I had making a baby all figured out. That part was fun. And the classes prepared me for the labor and delivery. However, I was not ready to be a dad. It would take me years to figure it all out. Balancing marriage, career, and parenting would prove to be the greatest challenge of my life. While I still struggle with balance every day, I have experienced major breakthroughs.

Later that night, Amy shared with me, "Ted, I hope you know things are going to change. The baby will need naps, regular feedings, and a schedule." Her beautiful eyes grabbed my attention, and I could feel her heart as she gently said, "*Everything* is going to change." Little did I know how right she was.

Now, I could share with you Amy's expectation from my perspective, but that just seems a little lopsided. So I have asked her to share with you her answer to the question "How will children change our lives?"

From Amy:

I thought children would fill a void in our home and complete our family. To me, they were the chapter right before "happily ever after."

I quickly learned that they take over space, schedules, money, and energy. I couldn't believe it, but they were actually creating voids, not filling them. Go figure! Our marriage was the first void felt.

The birth of our first child, Corynn, was a day filled with pain, anticipation, endurance, strength, and joy. Ted was so patient, and only a time or two did I wish he would stop asking me so many questions. Every friend I have ever asked about the birthing room knows those moments when you don't want to speak, be spoken to, or touched. Our poor husbands struggle in those brief moments.

My labor lasted about nine hours. (Okay, I'm back to not feeling too sorry for our husbands.) It was a long day. Labor started early in the morning and was over by lunch, but it felt like a week. As the doctor suited up, Ted and I held hands, prayed, and prepared for the little one God was giving us.

After the birth of our precious daughter, Corynn Mae, I entered the school of marriage and family reality, taking a full load of classes toward a degree in balance.

Breast-feeding did not go well with Corynn. I believed it was the healthiest option. For the first couple of weeks I fed Corynn for thirty to sixty minutes every couple of hours. We fed her for six to eight hours a day. I cried through most feedings. Exhaustion had drained my emotions. Ted would often sit speechless in the easy chair next to me. He had no idea what to say or do. Even if sexual intimacy were possible during the first six weeks after birth, for this first-time mom emotional intimacy was impossible.

When we went to the doctor for our two-month follow-up visit, we were told that Corynn was not gaining enough weight. I broke out in tears. I had spent nearly a third of my day feeding, and now I was being told that it was not enough. It was very frustrating and hurtful. Ted asked the doctor for suggestions. "You need to supplement the breast-feeding with formula," he said. But I wanted us to discuss this before we decided anything.

Later that night Ted prepared a bottle with the free formula we received in the hospital gift bag. I was hesitant, but the break from feeding sounded nice. What happened that night was the greatest gift I think a new mom ever receives: a full, uninterrupted night's sleep. When we woke up the next morning, Ted and I both jumped out of bed, fearing the worst. Our fears were relieved when we entered the room of a well-fed, rested baby girl.

The pressures placed on new parents can cause a deeply loving couple to put the marriage on hold. We waited seven years before children. We thought the delay would cement a bond that would last a lifetime. We wrestled with the question "How will having kids change our marriage?" We had completely different expectations on starting a family. Ted thought everything would remain the same. I knew everything would change. Ted wanted flexibility and life on the go. I wanted schedules and, dare I say, rigidity.

A whole new set of rules and schedules changed everything about the way we "did" life. Just like an airline must have a flight plan, Ted and I needed ours. With unforeseen turbulence, the flight had gotten a bit bumpy. For the first two months of Corynn's life, we did not have a flight plan. We had a birthing plan, but no parenting plan. But I was proud of Ted; he suggested a plan and I agreed. We went to work immediately by identifying the "bad weather" and navigating around it.

I am thrilled to report that we did create a plan that we believe helps us be great parents to our children and great lovers to each other. Ted is my best friend, and I love journeying with him.

The thoughts of a larger family conjured up images of family portraits, playgrounds, Disney World, and holidays. We were ready. Children would simply add to an already great life. Somewhere I read that children are "welcomed additions" to the family. That sounded good to me, so I went with that. It didn't take long for me to realize that kids change everything. Welcomed additions? At times it felt more like a hostile takeover as we morphed into a kid-centered home.

Before kids, Amy and I made love often, wherever and whenever we wanted in the house. Every room was a bedroom for us. We enjoyed much spontaneous lovemaking.

Kids changed everything. We had to schedule sex. That was new. We had to force ourselves to make love even when we were sleep deprived. We had sex less often and quickly became distracted lovers. Wondering if the baby would wake up, if she had a full stomach, or if she needed changing was always in the back of our minds. It was a frustrating season of life. But it was just that, a season.

You must guard your heart, marriage, and bed during this first phase of parenting. First of all, it really is a brief period of time that will pass quickly. You will not be sleep deprived forever. Your kids will grow up, go to the potty on their own in the middle of night (and wipe by themselves as well), and they will even be tall enough to get themselves a drink from the sink.

The changes children bring to the home do not have to destroy the frequency, performance, or endurance of your lovemaking. As you work through this book you will be given plenty of solid relational skills for your marriage. With those skills as the foundation, we will cover deep sexual intimacy in chapters 17 and 18. If sex has suffered in your home as a result of being a parent, hold on. Help is on the way.

Add your voice to the GPLL message . . .

Connect with us at www.greatparentslousylovers.com and watch the video podcast for chapter 3.

Post your thoughts, comments, and stories on our Web site. Here are some questions from chapter 3 to get you started on your journey to a couple-centered home:

- What were you expecting during your first pregnancy?
- What expectations for your family were met with no surprise?
- What expectations went unmet and now leave you frustrated?
- What pressures are on you as a parent that your spouse does not seem to understand?
- How can you adjust your expectations and better communicate those to your spouse and children?

CHANGE-IT-UP DATE:

Has parenting thrown you for a loop with all the
life changes it brought? In the spirit of change, do
something together that you've never done before.
This date can be as simple as going for a drive
somewhere you've never been, trying something
new on a restaurant menu, wearing something new,
double-dating with a couple you've never invited
out, stringing Christmas lights in the bedroom,
or watching a movie you've never seen. The
possibilities are endless. Change is good.

CHAPTER 4

THE KID-CENTERED HOME

You might be a Great Parent, Lousy Lover if one or more of your children sleep in your bed more than you do.

TED… Ten years in and three kids later, Jon was becoming a great parent and lousy lover. One evening he found himself sitting in the driveway, cell phone to ear, sharing with me a jaw-dropping statement. I'll never forget his call.

"Ted, give me one good reason to walk in this house," Jon insisted. "As soon as I walk in the door, Heather will hand me the kids and expect me to entertain them for the next four hours. To do anything else will show that I am a bad dad. I'm a good dad, but is it too much to ask for a little downtime from a hectic day?"

He went on to say, "I get that Heather is with the kids all day while I am at work, but our home is starting to feel more like shift work, rather than a couple raising children." What an observation. Heather devoted every waking moment of the daylight hours to the kids, and Jon was her replacement. Heather, like every hardworking mom on the planet, deserved time off. Jon, like every dutiful dad on the planet, deserves a break. What they were experiencing were the effects of a kid-centered home.

"Jon, do you guys spend any time alone at night?" I asked.

"We always intend to after the kids go to bed, but by that time we are too tired and mad to enjoy being together. We usually crash on the couch in silence."

I could have told him to suck it up and endure it for the next few years, but Jon and I have kids the exact same age, and I felt his pain. Been there, done that. So I avoided the minisermon and instead asked my favorite question, "How's that working for you?" Okay, I stole that line from Dr. Phil, but it is a great line. It is the best question to lead someone toward discovering the definition of insanity on their own: doing the same thing over and over again, expecting different results.

Jon answered my question by insisting, "That's life!"

"Really, Jon? You believe that there is nothing you can do to bring some balance to your life, marriage, and children?" I asked.

Here is where Jon and I are very much alike. We believed for a long time that you have to choose between life, marriage, and family. As though we can't have all three at once and be happy. When did we start choosing?

Without offending our wives, my friend Jon and I have spent much time together over the years trying to find freedom from the kid-centered home. But please don't hear that we don't love our kids. We love them very much! And don't hear that we are trying to get out of parenting. Not at all. We want to enjoy married life and raise great kids.

Like Jon, I am a guilt-prone parent. With my wife's permission, I can tell you that she is too. Our children have us right where they want us.

We thought we were ready for parenting. Amy and I prepared by reading books, taking classes, and visiting the doctor at each stage of the pregnancy. We traded in fun, sleek vehicles for more practical ones. We put a lot of furniture together with that cheap little hex tool they give you in the parts bag. The bottles were boiled, and the safety gate at the top of the stairs was installed.

For all of the joy we were anticipating as new parents, there was one thing we never prepared for: the vacuum of intimacy caused by guilt-prone parenting. Our anticipation was quickly replaced with fatigue and frustration. Our out-of-balance parenting started to destroy our marriage. We were at risk.

I made a huge mistake early on. I took my wife for granted and let her get worn down. We started living like the butler and the maid. To our kids, the house felt more like a hotel than a home. We offered them room service, shuttles, and amenities.

My solution was simple: endure the childhood years like

a concierge serving the guests. Then in our later years we'd retire, reconnect, and enjoy life once again. Bad idea! When I finally woke up, I knew something had to change.

Come to find out, we did not need to sacrifice intimacy in our marriage during the child-raising years. At first I did not believe it was possible to remain best friends and keep sexual intimacy hot. If you are just beginning with children and you desperately want to keep your love growing deeper, be encouraged. It is possible!

Amy struggles with the title of this book. She would prefer that it read Great Parents, Great Lovers. She is afraid that we will be pushing a knee-jerk reaction toward imbalance and encourage parents to back away from the blessing and responsibility of raising children. She makes a good point. We will heed her warning.

Our pursuit is in no way, shape, or form a desire to move away from great parenting. We simply want to keep from placing our marriages on the sacrificial altar of parenting.

———— 💜 ————

The Profile of a Kid-Centered Home

Great parents, lousy lovers create kid-centered homes. How do you know for sure if yours falls into this category? We believe there are four characteristics of a kid-centered home. We'll deal with the remedies to each of these in upcoming chapters, but for now we simply want to sketch the profile.

Great Parents, Lousy Lovers are guilt prone.

TED... My friend Kathy Lennon is a Boomer. She laughed at me one evening as I lamented my ineffectiveness as a parent.

With a chuckle she said, "Ted, the parents of today spend way too much time entertaining their kids. When I was growing up [with her Builder parents], they had this nifty invention called the playpen. Inside this playpen you would place toys and the children. You would drag this playpen from room to room as you did your household chores. If you had to do the dishes, you dragged it into the kitchen. To vacuum the living room, you dragged it in there, too. I don't know how you get anything done nowadays."

Amy and I have wrestled with the guilt factor when it comes to mowing the lawn, cleaning the house, and preparing meals. It only takes one of our children to come into the kitchen and say, "Do you have time to play with me?" With that, we feel as though we need to drop everything and entertain.

---------- 💔 ----------

You might be a guilt-prone parent if you . . .

- skip a date night because the kids are crying for you to stay home;
- go on a date, but call home from the driveway right after you leave;
- bring home gifts for the kids after the date;

- promise them you'll do something special with them the next day;
- ask your kids permission to go somewhere or do something;
- buy them something from the dollar bin to make up for all the errands you need to run;
- invite them to make decisions on every activity, meal, errand, or vacation.

Guilt-prone gestures communicate, "I'll make it up to you." Since when did we need to make up for our marriage? Giving our children a mommy and daddy who love each other and spend time with each other is better than anything you can wrap and place under a tree. Stop apologizing for spending time with your spouse.

Great Parents, Lousy Lovers tend to be permissive.

Permissive parents tend to be warm, supporting people but weak in establishing and enforcing rules and limits for their children. One of the major reasons some parents are too permissive is an inner fear that they may damage their children if they are too strict.

On the positive side, permissive parents are strong in the area of support. Effective parents realize that a certain degree of permissiveness is healthy. That means accepting that kids will be kids, a clean shirt will not stay clean for long, running will almost always be preferable to walking, a tree is for climbing, and a mirror for making faces. It means accepting that children have the right to childlike feelings and dreams. That kind of permissiveness gives a child confidence and an increasing capacity to express his or her thoughts and feelings.

Overpermissiveness leads to a kid-centered home. It allows for undesirable acts such as bullying and destruction of property.

————— ♥ —————

You might be a permissive parent if you have ever said . . .
- "Well, okay. You can stay up late this time. I know how much you like this program."
- "You didn't hear me call you for dinner. Well, that's all right. Sit down. I don't want you eating a cold dinner."
- "Please don't get angry with me. You're making a scene."
- "I've asked three times; don't make me ask again."

Permissive parenting results in children who sense that they are in the driver's seat and can play the parent accordingly. Children develop a feeling of insecurity in a permissive household, like leaning against a wall that appears to be firm but topples. They may have little self-respect because they have not learned to control and master certain personal disciplines. That is the direct result of standards that are not firm and rules that are manipulated.

Kid-centered homes misunderstand the parent-child bond.

TED... I love it when a mom comes up to me at a wedding and says, "I don't feel like I am losing a daughter today—I feel like I'm gaining a son." My response is simple and blunt: "Nope! You are losing a daughter." That perspective—that one must leave in order to cleave—is the key to launching a young couple into oneness in marriage. Your parents and your kids can chip away at that bond.

Ephesians 5:31 says, "For this cause shall a man leave his father and mother, and shall cleave to his wife; and the two shall become one flesh" (ASV). That word for "cleave" is translated as "glue" in modern Hebrew. A married man and woman are designed to become glue, but that natural bond cannot form if they are still cleaving to Mom and Dad.

That glue can also begin to dissolve when we attempt to develop a stronger bond with our kids rather than our spouse. Here's where we will make some of our readers mad. God never intended the bond between parent and child to be as strong, let alone stronger, than the bond between husband and wife. Ouch! God created the bond between man and wife to be stronger than that between parent and child.

Corynn will often ask me, "Daddy, do you love me as much as Mommy?" Tough question to answer. Amy always will look at me with a "How do you answer that, Ted?" face.

You may answer that quickly and easily, but I always pause because I want her to know that one day she will leave our home and go out on her own. My bond with Corynn is different from my bond with Amy.

———————— ♥ ————————

God says in Genesis 2:24, "For this reason a man will leave his father and mother and be united to his wife, and they will become one flesh." God is not talking about Adam and Eve's marriage, because Adam and Eve didn't have a mother or father to leave. Nobody walked Eve down the aisle. He's talking about the pattern for marriages to come.

Jesus restates Genesis 2:24 in Matthew 19:5 and expands on it in verse 6: "So they are no longer two, but one. Therefore what God has joined together, let man not separate." God has united man and wife in a glue relationship. He doesn't describe the parent-child relationship that way. You see, God did not design us to have kid-centered marriages. Kids grow up and leave. You and your spouse are united for a lifetime. You are not united to your kids for a lifetime.

Kid-centered homes fill the margin and lack rhythm.

The kid-centered home is chaotic, scattered, fragmented, distracted, and overloaded. *Margin* is the fuel for healthy pace and rhythm. Margin says, "I have a free thirty minutes, so I am going to leave it open to do nothing." You don't need to fill the margin with another activity. Margin believes that doing nothing is not a waste of time. It is an opportunity to refuel and relax. Whether they know it or not, our kids are crying out for margin. *Rhythm* creates an ebb and flow that kids can come to expect throughout the week. They know there will be regular rest and periods of downtime between activities.

The best way to illustrate this is by picturing your family life like a balloon. Every activity, sporting event, school function, errand, and meal is one puff of air into the balloon. Our work gets a couple of good puffs. Every scheduled task gets a puff.

Here's where we stink: letting air out of the balloon. Letting air out is building margin. God's desire for your family is not a fragmented, scattered, or chaotic pace. I never hear anybody set out to say, "I want to live a chaotic life. I'm running at such a pace that I don't even know how to stop." But all we do is continue to fill our lives; we don't work in any margin, and we don't understand rhythms. Because God cares for your soul and mine, he has given us the Sabbath. We'll look closer at margin and the Sabbath in chapters 6 and 7. The Sabbath is God's way of helping you and me let a little air out of the balloon. Actually, it's a command to let the air out.

One last question to answer: Who is in charge of your family balloon? It sounds like a silly question, but the kid-centered home would have the kids determining how much air to let in, and they would rarely choose to let any out. A great parent takes charge of the balloon, determining what to allow in and when it is necessary to let some out. That discipline is part of being an adult. Children must learn it with age.

Taking back your life and marriage from the kid-centered home is one of the greatest gifts you can give your children. Just like Jon and Heather, and Tim and Lisa, whom you'll meet in the next chapter, we must not let our marriages slip away. Let's get back to the fun, play, and laughter we experienced in our youth.

Add your voice to the GPLL message . . .

Connect with us at www.greatparentslousylovers.com and watch the video podcast for chapter 4.

Post your thoughts, comments, and stories on our Web site. Here are some questions from chapter 4 to get you started on your journey to a couple-centered home:

- Are you a guilt-prone parent? How does that play out on a typical day in your home?

- Does your guilt lead you toward a permissive parenting style? What are some of your permissive-parent statements?

- Are you willing to begin teaching your kids the differences between the parent-child and husband-wife bonds? How will you word it in an age-appropriate way?

- Think through the rhythm of your day. What about your rhythm is healthy? What parts are unhealthy?

STRESS-FREE DATE:

You and your beloved deserve time to connect away from the scene of the stress. Get out of the house for at least twenty-four consecutive hours . . . alone together. Where there's a will there's a way to make this happen regardless of responsibilities or budget. Ask for and accept help from family and friends to make a getaway a reality.

CHAPTER 5

CHOOSING BETWEEN LIFE & WIFE

You might be a Great Parent, Lousy Lover if you have ever responded to a friend's engagement announcement by saying, "Are you sure you want to go through with this? Think it through long and hard."

Let the wife make the husband glad to come home; and let him make her sorry to see him leave. ‖ MARTIN LUTHER

GARY... Every January in Branson, our church hosts a Love and Laughter Getaway for couples. We take over the Chateau on the Lake resort and invite couples from all around the country to a great time of loving and laughing. We get a couple of local comedians, Ted and I talk a little on marriage, and we enjoy the amenities of the hotel. The goal of this getaway is to stay far away from anything that would resemble a husband-bashing seminar or a "woman, give your husband more sex" conference. We want an entire weekend when couples can become doers of Ecclesiastes 9:9 and enjoy life with each other.

We have been amazed at the turnout and impact of this

annual getaway. Story after story gets back to us about how it radically changed couples. Seriously? A weekend of laughter, fun, and play changes lives? Yep! Do you know who needs this event the most? Parents! You know most of us forget how to enjoy life and each other. All types of parents show up. From parents of toddlers to parents of college students (i.e., empty nesters), they all come back year after year to be reminded that fun, laughter, and play must never leave the home.

Tim and Lisa, from St. Louis, are huge fans of this getaway. Married for twenty years, they are now empty nesters who had nothing left for each other once the kids left home. They stopped enjoying each other fifteen or so years ago. In December 2007, they were done. The kids were out of the house, and either Tim or Lisa would soon be gone too. They fell into the pattern we see in so many Boomer couples. They worked so hard to raise kids that they forgot how to enjoy each other. There was nothing left of their marriage.

Ted met Tim and Lisa in August 2009. I had the privilege to watch Ted in one of his finer pastoral moments. Actually, it didn't start out that way, but it ended up great. On this warm summer Sunday, I watched as the cutest couple with smiles from ear to ear introduced themselves.

"You both sure look happy," Ted said as he introduced me.

"Life is great," Tim said. "You don't have a clue who we are, do you?"

"I'm sorry," Ted said with a deer-in-the-headlights look. "Where are you from?" That is always his standard deflecting question.

"We're from St. Louis, and we are here today because you are renewing our vows at the end of the second service," Tim said.

Ted had completely forgotten. Oops! There's nothing like watching a friend drowning and standing there helpless. He was sinking fast. Tim's and Lisa's smiles started to fade. But his recovery was masterful. Woodland Hills gives Ted a month off every summer for a study break, and this was his first Sunday back. Things were a little cloudy. Then it hit him. He tried to wing it, but he was caught.

"Can't wait," Ted said. What they said next floored both of us.

"Ted and Gary, the Love and Laughter Getaway saved our marriage!" Lisa said through tears.

Inside I thought, *You've got to be kidding me. That crazy little event we host with a couple of comedians saved your marriage?* This event is such a whirlwind for me every year. It is nonstop laughter, and I usually walk away thinking, *That was fun, but I don't know if we taught anything.* The more we do that crazy event, the more I am realizing the need for couples to laugh, play, and have fun together.

"That weekend changed everything for us. We remembered laughing together years earlier and had no idea why or when the laughter ever left our home," Lisa said.

Tim and Lisa sat through both services. When the auditorium cleared out after the second service, our worship pastor played a little tinkly music and invited Tim and Lisa to step up on stage with Ted, and they renewed their vows right on the spot. They held hands as they faced each other and through many tears apologized for letting their marriage slip away. They recommitted to a lifetime of serving and enjoying one another. Our softy worship pastor was choking back a few tears. They read and prayed that God would renew a bond that was lost to their kid-centered home.

What a challenge to empty nesters and a warning to my Buster friends. When did couples stop enjoying each other and start enduring each other? God did not intend for my wife and kids to be a part of the grind. Let's dig deeper together to learn how and when couples like Tim and Lisa lost their marriage to a kid-centered home.

Most people would point to Ephesians 5 as the main marriage text of the Bible. To do so overlooks a major nugget in the Old Testament. I get that we are to lay down our lives for our wives, guys, but I think God never intended for us to choose between life and wife. Solomon says that we can, and should, enjoy both. In chapter 1 of Ecclesiastes, life is portrayed like a big grinder. Verse 4 says, "Generations come and generations go, but the earth remains forever." We are born into this grinder, and the churning begins. We face hard times and challenges. No one on earth knows about this grinder better than parents.

However, this is the best part: God did not give me my spouse as part of the grind, but to help me through it. That's a paradigm shift from most modern marriage teaching. I have taught for years that God did not give me my spouse to make me happy, but to make me holy. While God does use marriage to refine us, when taken exclusively, that belief system leaves out the flip side from the teachings of Solomon.

At the other end of the book we read that we will ultimately die: "When the keepers of the house tremble, and the strong men stoop . . ." (Ecclesiastes 12:3). We become fragile, and our bodies start breaking down. Oh boy, can I relate to this. After a heart attack and kidney transplant, I now have the full-time job of staying alive.

"When the grinders cease because they are few [we lose our teeth], and those looking through the windows grow dim [our glasses get thicker and thicker; we begin to lose our eyesight]; when the doors to the street are closed and the sound of grinding fades; when men rise up at the sound of birds, but all their songs grow faint . . ." (Ecclesiastes 12:3-4).

We get up at the sound of the birds, but Solomon says there's a problem: We can't enjoy them because our hearing is going.

"When men are afraid of heights and of dangers in the streets" (verse 5), we then develop fear. Many seniors won't drive at night because of night blindness.

"When the almond tree blossoms" (verse 5), our hair begins to turn gray.

The last thing that we read about is this: "And the grasshopper drags himself along and desire no longer is stirred" (verse 5). You're thinking, *Let me see if I think I know what that means.* It means exactly what you think it does. Sex is over. The grasshopper is dragging. Sexual desire is no longer stirred. I thought for the longest time . . . *Geico has a gecko.*

I think Viagra needs a grasshopper in a little white sweater with a big blue "V."

I love when Ted asks his wife, "Amy, will you still love me when my grasshopper's dragging?" And do you know what she says? I kid you not, she says, "I think I'll be all right." She then asks, "What are you going to do, Ted, when your grasshopper starts dragging?"

He answers, "The Lord can take me home. Life will just be over." You laugh, but that's what the Bible says.

"Then man goes to his eternal home and mourners go about the streets" (verse 5).

So there is the outline of Ecclesiastes: Life is hard, then you die. Encouraged yet? But wait, there's more. Thank you, Father. You and I have a responsibility in the daily grind of work and kids to have a smokin' hot marriage. Ecclesiastes 9:7 commands us, "Go, eat your food with gladness, and drink your wine with a joyful heart." In the midst of the grind, you still need to enjoy life. You still need to find those moments when you enjoy one another and you spend time laughing together. Don't throw those moments out the window because life is difficult. Those moments are gifts from God.

Then look at my favorite verse of the whole book. Verse 9 says, "Enjoy life with your wife." Enjoy finding times of joy and play and laughter. Solomon says to find them with your wife. Enjoy life with your wife. This is the only place where it says this in the Bible. Proverbs 5:18-19 says, "Rejoice in the wife of your youth. . . . May her breasts satisfy you always."

But it doesn't say enjoy *life* with your wife. You and I are not to choose between enjoying life or enjoying our spouse, as if both can't be done. God never intended for your spouse to be a part of your earthly grind; he gave you your spouse as a comfort in the grind.

I love hearing guys tell me, "I had all sorts of plans, dreams, and goals for the future, but then I got married" or "My wife and I had all sorts of plans, dreams, and goals for the future, but then we had kids." Let me give you the Greek/Hebrew term for those statements: hogwash! Your spouse is not brought into your life to kill your play, dreams, goals, and fun. Kids are not brought into your life to be killjoys either. Throughout the rest of the book we will learn together how to balance and enjoy life with our spouse and family.

Maybe you grew up in a home where your mom and dad did not enjoy each other. They may have stayed married, but they annoy, put up with, or are indifferent to one another. Now your outlook on what marriage could be is bleak. You have no hope for the future. No hope for a great marriage.

Can I just add this hopeful and encouraging thought for you? My wife, Norma, has supported every dream, hope, and job I ever had. Somehow we managed to play, laugh, and enjoy our life together all the years our kids were in the house. Our family camped together at least two times a month, and she and I totally enjoyed each other and our kids together. Now that we're in our seventies, we are still laughing, enjoying each other, adjusting to the major changes, and keeping our eyes on Christ. His words live within us today just as they did when our kids were with us. Now we get to enjoy our grandkids—and we still enjoy each other. Just last week, I made a major shift in my life: I turned over the administration of our ministry to my wife because she is gifted at it and loves it. I still speak and write, but she is totally in charge of running the ministry we built together. After she has supported me so much over the past forty years, now I'm enjoying supporting her, too!

TED... This hopelessness for a great marriage is leading young people today to delay marriage. Many teens and young adults I hang out with believe they have to choose between life and marriage.

Justin's text was my first ever digital engagement announcement. He wrote, "Just got engaged. She said yes. Can u believe it? Can't wait! Will u do the wedding?"

I responded with, "You'll love being married! It's gr8! You r a fantastic couple. Proud of u J and J!"

Justin and Jocelyn are the classic couple. He's twenty-three. She's twenty-one. Justin is a professional magician who has graced the stages of Branson, Vegas, and countless cruise liners. Jocelyn is finishing up her schooling to become a counselor. They dated for six months prior to their engagement and have their whole life ahead of them.

As Justin's friend more than his pastor, I heard him mention the big "M" word months before he asked Jocelyn. I asked all the appropriate questions: Is she a follower of Jesus?

Does she have a temper? Have you known her long enough to see what really sets her off? You know, the basic "Should I walk down the aisle?" type of stuff.

A few weeks after their engagement announcement, Amy and I had Justin and Jocelyn over for dinner and their first premarital session. I quickly learned that I would not be teaching Justin a whole lot that night. His excitement for marriage oozed out of every pore of his body. He had already attended two marriage conferences and read half a dozen books prior to popping the question. I don't know whether to call him a teacher's pet, poster child, hopeless romantic, or marriage dweeb. But nevertheless, he was eager and excited. Most couples anticipate the wedding. It is rare to meet a young couple excited about paying bills, taking on a mortgage, and balancing life and work, but Justin and Jocelyn were that couple.

After dinner Justin performed a few table magic tricks for our kids, and then we dived right into it.

He said, "Ted, you were the only one excited for us when we announced our engagement."

"What?" I said.

"Yeah, our parents encouraged us to not rush things and give it a little more time. Our friends couldn't understand why we would want to give up our freedom in singleness. You were the only one who jumped up and down for us."

Justin's friends and family are not an anomaly. I am beginning to feel the same sentiment around the country. My alma mater, Liberty University, invites me back to speak each year at convocation. My returns to that conservative, evangelical coed world have opened my ears to a tone among twenty-somethings that goes something like this: "I need to protect my future from marriage." It comes out in statements like

- "We have so many divorces in our society today because couples are marrying too early."
- "I want to settle into my career before settling down in marriage."
- "My girlfriend and I have different career pursuits, and we're afraid that marriage right now could sabotage both our futures."
- "I know the right guy will come along, but I'm not looking or pursuing any serious relationships."
- "I'm not ready for marriage."
- "I was ready to marry him, but he wasn't ready."
- "He needs to figure out what he is going to do in life before we take our relationship to the next level."

Did you pick up on the tone? It's not mean or frustrated, but it casts a shadow on marriage. But is marriage the problem? I don't believe so. The bigger issue is maturity. I can confess to you that I was not the right person for Amy Freitag when we walked down the aisle, but I've been working on becoming the right person. And we definitely did not have our future all figured out before we married. We're thirteen years in and still figuring that out. That's what makes it so great. We are living out marriage as an adventure, not a choice between the two.

Add your voice to the GPLL message . . .

Connect with us at www.greatparentslousylovers.com and watch the video podcast for chapter 5.

Post your thoughts, comments, and stories on our Web site. Here are some questions from chapter 5 to get you started on your journey to a couple-centered home:

- Tough question: Do you ever feel as though you are missing out on something in life due to marriage or kids?

- What have you accomplished as a result of being married that you could not have accomplished while single?

- What was the toughest part of being single?

- What was the best part of being single?

- What has been the toughest part of being married?

- What has been the best part of being married?

NATURE DATE:

Ever notice the rejuvenating power of nature? Go for a walk together in the early morning or the starlit evening. Find a secluded park bench, a shady picnic place, a soothing rest spot with a water view, or even your own comfy deck furniture to pause together and appreciate God's beautiful creation.

CHAPTER 6

HOW TO ADD
MORE TIME IN YOUR DAY

You might be a Great Parent, Lousy Lover if your idea of a date night is watching the kids play on the playground at Chick-fil-A.

TED... A few months back I had to rush home and get cleaned up before the kids' soccer practice. I zipped to the restroom (funny how we still call it a restroom, funnier how we rush to it) and noticed we were out of toilet paper. Does that set anyone else off besides me? I ran to another bathroom to find the Charmin. Notice I didn't go and get a fresh roll for the one bathroom. I grabbed a roll and left it on the bathtub nearby because I did not have three or four seconds to place it on the holder.

Later that night as the kids were taking a bath, that roll of toilet paper fell into the bathtub. My daughter, in the kindness and goodness of her heart, flushed the entire roll of double-quilted, double-roll toilet paper, the finest money can buy (nothing but the best for the Cunninghams' hind ends). She came into my office and announced, "Daddy, the toilet is overflowing." I rushed into the bathroom, and sure enough she was right.

I did what most of you would do. I said, "That's okay." Yeah, right! After I overreacted, we got the plunger and cleaned things up.

Corynn felt awful. I will never forget her words. She said, "I'm stupid, ain't I?"

I said, "Corynn, you are not stupid. Daddy reacted and had to get the water cleaned up and tank unplugged. No way are you stupid. But we don't say *ain't*." Just kidding— I didn't say that.

The next morning I woke up, and it just gripped me again. So I went over to Corynn, who was sitting on the couch, and said, "Corynn, can I talk to you about last night and about the toilet?"

The first words out of her mouth were "Daddy, I said I was sorry."

"Corynn," I explained, "I want you to hear this again. I apologized last night, and I am going to apologize again. Daddy overreacted. This house means nothing to me. Toilets are not that important. But you are so important to Daddy.

"Daddy needs to not react so much to this type of stuff," I said. "Just to prove it, do you want to go flush another roll of toilet paper down the toilet? Let's do it; just me and you.

We'll cut it off in pieces and maybe do more than one flush to try to get the whole thing down."

All of this chaos, frustration, offense, and apology were the direct result of hurry. We run too fast. It has been said that hurry kills the soul. It also kills the family.

A. W. Tozer once wrote, "Time is a resource that is non-renewable and nontransferable. You cannot store it, slow it up, hold it up, divide it up or give it up. You can't hoard it up or save it for a rainy day—when it's lost it is unrecoverable. When you kill time, remember that it has no resurrection."

God wants us to enjoy a life in which time is not the enemy. We say things like "I wish I could have more time," "Sorry, but we're out of time," "Where has the time gone?" and "Time sure flies." We like to max out our lives and make the most of every minute and opportunity. We squeeze out the margin to get the most out of life.

But time is nothing more than an investment. We tend to treat it more like a consumer good. Investing is all about saving rather than spending. How we use our family time today affects how well tomorrow will go. Billy Graham, in a message on time, said, "More than seventy-five years ago Henry Luce wanted a name, in just one word, for a weekly newsmagazine that would describe the passing events of the day. He chose the word *time*. The Bible says, 'The days of our lives are seventy years' (Psalm 90:10, NKJV). Time is a mystery. We sense its passing in our consciousness. We measure its progress with delicately adjusted instruments. We mark its flight and read the record it leaves behind." He went on to say, "To the Christian, time has a moral significance and a spiritual meaning. . . . What are we doing with it? Are we frittering it away, letting it slip through our fingers, squandering it in wanton waste? Or are we treasuring it, using it to maximum advantage, filling every minute with sixty seconds' worth of service to God?"

Our kids tend to get the leftovers of our time. How we invest our time is linked to our energy level. A fast pace wears us down and spends the time. The pace at which we run drains our tanks, and usually our kids get the fumes. Once they exhaust the fumes, our spouse is left with nothing.

Speed is the enemy of intimacy. Even if my schedule is not packed and my e-mails are all answered, I find I have a hurried spirit. I remember the time when I was running out of the house going nowhere important and Amy said she had something to share with me. I responded with "Talk fast." She said, "I'll wait until you can listen slow." Ouch.

In his book, *The 7 Habits of Highly Effective People*, Stephen Covey writes, "Time management is a misleading concept. You can't really manage time. You can't delay it, speed it up, save it or lose it. No matter what you do time keeps moving forward at the same rate. The challenge is not to manage time, but to manage ourselves." Great advice for us parents. We can't manage time, but we can manage our homes. We can manage our pace.

The Bible never uses the term "time management." Instead, it speaks of "redeeming" the time. Pacing ourselves, rather than controlling time. Paul writes, "See then that you walk circumspectly, not as fools but as wise, redeeming the time, because the days are evil" (Ephesians 5:15-16, NKJV).

The most important thing to know about time is that it is limited. Armed with that truth, the most important question you and I must begin asking is "What am I going to say no to?" Delayed gratification is saying no to something now in the hopes of something better later.

Remember the balloon from chapter 4 that represents your family's time? Larger families do not have larger balloons. Smaller families do not have smaller balloons. We each get twenty-four hours. When it comes to time, the playing field is level for every family. We control the flow of air in and out. When our family schedule is at full capacity, how do we let the air out? Are you ready for the secret? It is simpler than I originally thought.

Maintaining Margin and Rhythm

Our marriages need it. Our children crash and burn without it. We are less productive when we don't get enough of it. Too much of it and some might consider us lazy. Know what it is? It is rest, letting the air out of the balloon.

Margin means room to breathe. It's a reserve. We have all been there when we are driving on fumes and can't find a gas station. The panic and anxiety set in, and we feel helpless. As we discussed previously, margin keeps a little fuel in the tank at all times. It refuses to run on fumes. It does not rush from one errand or meeting to another. It doesn't stretch the balloon to the point of bursting.

Margin is the space between your load and your limit. As a young dad and pastor, I have often allowed my load to exceed my limit, saying yes to every request for a meeting or counseling appointment, yes to every invitation to speak, yes to every party or meal invite. It wasn't until a much older and wiser pastor asked me, "Who is holding a gun to your head?" that I woke up to how I was living. He taught me that if I don't get ahold of my schedule, someone else will. I am a much happier pastor, husband, and dad because I learned the big word *No!* Ahh . . . I can hear the balloon deflating.

Being marginless is when you allow your load to exceed your limit. The key word there is *you*, not *load* or *limit*. Admit it, when you first read that line, *load* and *limit* jumped out at you. You missed the *you*. We must take personal responsibility for the way we invest our time, the amount of margin we allow, and the rest we get. We are responsible for our load. Don't allow your load to be dictated by anyone else. After all, only you know your limit. There's not another person on the planet who understands your limit. You feel when you've had enough people time. You know when you better get alone and re-center before you go all "postal." No one knows you better than you. Your limit is what determines your necessary margin.

Marginless is being twenty minutes late to gymnastics because you were fifteen minutes late getting out of the store because you were ten minutes late picking up the kids from school because there was an unexpected traffic accident. Good "time redeeming" leaves a little margin in your daily plan. We all need margin and rest.

Since when did I start thinking I was better than God? He rested after creating for six days. Jesus ministered, and then he rested. He told the disciples, "Hey, let's break away from the pack, and let's just chill for a while. Let's reenergize, recoup, rest our bodies and our emotions. Let's just take some downtime so we can be more effective when we come back to the job, when we come back to the ministry." Okay, that's our paraphrase of Mark 6:30-31, but you get the point.

God knew we would rebel against the whole idea of rest, so he had to command it: "Remember the Sabbath day by keeping it holy" (Exodus 20:8). *Holy* means set apart. We are not to treat the Sabbath like every other day of the week. It needs a different rhythm. "Six days you shall labor and do all your work" (verse 9). For six days God says to work and provide for your family. He wants us to be productive. And he has given us the Sabbath to make us more productive. "But the seventh day is a Sabbath to the LORD your God. On it you shall not do any work" (verse 10). You need to slow down the pace of yourself, your spouse, and your children, and you need to find rest and relax.

A Sabbath does not mean a day off. It means a day of rest. Jesus said, "The Sabbath was made to meet the needs of people, and not people to meet the requirements of the Sabbath" (Mark 2:27, NLT). The Sabbath is a gift to us. This, my friend, is for your benefit.

Say no to time robbers.

One story that has always inspired me is of Ken Griffey Jr., the dad, not the baseball player. Several years ago, Ken Griffey Jr. was invited to the Players Choice Awards, where he was to be named player of the decade. His award was to be given on national television. He beat out players like Barry Bonds and Mark McGwire. But when he found out when the award was to be given, he declined to attend. He had something more important to do. His five-year-old son, Trey, was playing in his first baseball game, and Ken wasn't going to miss it. Hip, hip, hooray! Proud of you, Ken.

He said no to fame and the spotlight of others. Most of our *yes* answers are driven by what others have asked for and how we will be perceived. Sure, we may not be receiving any awards for our performance, but we look for the approval of others.

The demands and expectations of others are the greatest of all time robbers. As a pastor I can admit that the church can be quite guilty of this. Woodland Hills is a family church, and one of the things we have guarded more than anything else is family time. It would be crazy to say we support the family and then ask people to be at the church four or five times a week. But here's the rub. Everything we ask our congregation to take part in involves a great ministry opportunity. Feed the poor, attend a Bible study, serve the recovery program, teach kids on Sunday morning—all great opportunities, but not opportunities anyone needs to say yes to every time.

We are saying no to really good stuff. But we say *no* for a bigger and better *yes*. No matter what your role, be careful of the time robbers.

Number your days.

Psalm 90 is the only psalm of all 150 that was written by Moses. After Moses was on the run, God sent him back to Egypt. After talking with Pharaoh, Moses led the nation of Israel out of Egypt. Then one of the greatest miracles happened. God parted the Red Sea so the people could cross to the other side. They had a worship service, and then a couple of days later they were hungry and started whining again. Moses put up with this for an entire generation (see Exodus 2–17). Sound familiar? Moses was a stressed-out parent looking for a renewed sense of purpose.

At some point all of us need a renewed sense of purpose. "God, remind me again why I'm doing what I'm doing. Why did I have children, again? Remind me that there is actual purpose beyond the daily grind."

"Lord, you have been our dwelling place throughout all generations," Moses wrote (Psalm 90:1). In other words, "God, as we look back over the generations, even during our most rebellious and complaining times, you were there; you were the one we turned to. When we were hungry, we came to you. When we were lost, confused, in a daze, we came to you. You have always been the resting place for us."

He goes on to verse 2, and this is where we look at God's eternal existence as the source of our comfort: "Before the mountains were born or you brought forth the earth and the world, from everlasting to everlasting you are God." God is the One. Man does not set the course of human history; God does. He is the One in whom every generation finds rest.

A *lament* psalm declares three simple but huge statements: "God, I am hurting, the enemy is winning, and it seems that you don't care." Well, Psalm 90 is a lament from Daddy Moses struggling with his kids. Our friend Kevin Leman once said in a message at our church: "I have seen the enemy, and they are small."

Don't lose sight of the eternal goal as you spend time with your kids. You are investing in eternity more than you are preparing them for college. "The length of our days is seventy years"—that's how much time you have, so plan your time wisely—"or eighty, if we have the strength" (Psalm 90:10). I like that. If you are strong enough and you can live it and you muscle through it, you might get eighty. "Yet their span is but trouble and sorrow, for they quickly pass, and we fly away" (verse 10).

Verse 12 goes on to say, "Teach us to number our days aright, that we may gain a heart of wisdom." Verse 14 says, "Satisfy us in the morning with your unfailing love, that we may sing for joy and be glad all our days." Verse 15 continues, "Make us glad for as many days as you have afflicted us, for as many years as we have seen trouble." We are to be intentional with our days. Even though life is hard, we can choose to learn from our struggles. Learning and growing are the antidote to stress and anxiety.

How important are redeeming the time and numbering our days? To realize the value of one year, ask a student who failed a grade. To realize the value of one month, ask a mother who gave birth to a premature baby. How valuable is an hour? Ask the businessman whose flight was delayed by that much, causing him to miss an important business deal. How about one minute? Ask the man who had the heart attack in a restaurant and was saved by an EMT proficient in CPR who happened to be sitting at the next table. Does a second mean much to you? It does to the person who barely missed a head-on collision with an oncoming car. Surely a millisecond isn't a big deal—unless you're the Olympic swimmer who missed qualifying by six-tenths.

Time is the most precious commodity you have. Benjamin Franklin put it best when he said, "Do not squander time, for it is the stuff life is made of." I would add it is the stuff family is made of.

Add your voice to the GPLL message . . .

Connect with us at www.greatparentslousylovers.com and watch the video podcast for chapter 6.

Post your thoughts, comments, and stories on our Web site. Here are some questions from chapter 6 to get you started on your journey to a couple-centered home:

- Describe the pace of your home [check all that apply]:
  - ❑ Frantic
  - ❑ Balanced

- ❑ Healthy
- ❑ Unhealthy
- ❑ Relaxed
- ❑ Procrastinating
- ❑ Frustrated
- ❑ Exhausted
- ❑ Empty
- ❑ Full

• What needs more time and attention in your home?

• Name three things that you need to say no to this week to manage your pace.

• When you start managing your pace, who may try to put you on a guilt trip for saying no? Brainstorm what you will say to help that person understand.

PACE YOUR DATES:

Think you're too busy to date? You're too busy *not* to date! The more you have pulling at you, the more you need to create opportunities to connect as a couple so those to-dos don't pull you away from each other. How about a date to fit every schedule?

- *The daily microdate:* Steal a hug and kiss while passing in the hall.
- *The weekly minidate:* Turn off the TV and talk for an hour.
- *The semimonthly dinner date:* Have dinner for two, home or preferably away, with no kids.
- *The monthly "up-date":* Create heart-to-heart time for encouragement and evaluation of your relationship.
- *The yearly getaway:* Spend at least one night away together each year.
- *The celebration date:* Don't miss a chance to celebrate the biggies . . . fifth/tenth/fifteenth anniversaries, major accomplishments, and milestones—these are worthy of at least a long weekend away, if not longer.

BUILDING MARGIN

You might be a Great Parent, Lousy Lover if you are consistently late to events and activities because you are coming from other kid events and activities.

TED... The Hall family rarely took a day off, let alone a day of rest. Sure, Michael and Ali took their four kids on great vacations, but rest was hard for them. It took a Crayola drawing by their five year old to shock Michael into one of the biggest decisions of his life. Their family pace, led by Dad, was out of control. And this innocent drawing led Michael to make an abrupt, radical, and brave change that makes most of us ask, "Is he out of his mind?"

Michael was a type-A, hard-charging, successful CEO. The pace of his job meant acquire, build, sell, then move on to the next opportunity. And travel was a big part of the job.

One night Michael came home on the last flight out of New York and arrived to a sleeping house. He unloaded his bags and headed to the kitchen for a snack. As he sat down at a dimly lit table, he noticed a drawing by his five-year-old daughter, Madie. The drawing depicted the Hall family: Mom, Dad, and kids. But their arrangement on the sketch brought Michael to tears. Mom, Toben, Madie, Lowden, and Marley were all holding hands on a sage green stretch of grass under a sea blue sky. Next to the sun was an airplane in a lightly shaded pearl white. Michael was waving to his family from thirty-two thousand feet.

Right then and there Michael knew that the pace of his life and family must change. They needed a break from the pace of the Joneses. Rest was the only thing that could save their family. He sold his company, and they packed up and moved to a new state, where Michael was mentored in marriage, fatherhood, and business by a wise friend.

Let's look at this backward and personalized: You have no time or energy for your spouse because you used up your fumes on the kids because you played with them when you got home to make up for being gone on that weeklong business trip because you had to close the next deal because you want to give your kids everything you never had. Interesting, what starts out as a desire to better your family destroys you.

I like saying this prayer at the beginning of our family Sabbath that resigns me as the general manager of the universe: "Father in heaven, you created the earth in six days and you rested on the seventh. You created the earth in a week, and you did it all without me. I can take a day off, and I'm going to have to put the world back in your hands." I wonder if that little prayer once a week will keep me from a crash and burn. Maybe a decision to walk away from the job is not necessary if I could learn to build margin and manage the rhythm of my life, career, and home.

The Sabbath creates rhythm, builds margin, and prevents burnout. Let's look at several practical ways your home can move away from hurry and run toward rest.

GARY... I'd like to interject an idea to dads and moms who have been given extra talent and intelligence from God. Ted is one of those rare individuals who is gifted in so many different areas. In my mind, he could "manage the world." But I get to watch him set boundaries and say no to some people who would like to get his advice or utilize his skills for their own projects. He helps people out, but he's selective about it because he knows he only has so many hours in a day. At times in my own life when I've been overly busy, I've had to do what so many other parents have done—look seriously at my time commitments and cut things out to spend more time with my wife and kids. I used to ask God to provide jobs in which I could earn enough to take care of my family and still have plenty of time to spend with them. I would tell God, "Please don't let me pastor a church and take care of all the people and their kids but lose my own children." He was faithful in answering that prayer.

Choose a Day

Some people misunderstand the purpose and intent of the Ten Commandments. Since technically, to the Orthodox

Jew, the Sabbath is on Saturday and we worship on Sunday, which day do we choose? In Revelation 1:10, John refers to this day, the first day of the week, as the Lord's Day. In the New Testament, first-century Christians no longer observed Saturday as the Sabbath. Instead, in commemoration and celebration of the Lord's resurrection, Sunday became their day of rest.

"One man considers one day more sacred than another; another man considers every day alike. Each one should be fully convinced in his own mind. He who regards one day as special, does so to the Lord" (Romans 14:5-6). Don't make the day of the week the issue; the issue is *rest*.

Do the Ten Commandments still apply to us today? Can we still obey and follow the fourth commandment (see Exodus 20:8)? Absolutely. Jesus said he did not come to abolish the law, but to fulfill it (see Matthew 5:17). We are no longer tied to a day, but rest is still the issue. God still wants you to have a day when you rest your mind, emotions, and body.

The great commandments are now to love the Lord your God with all your heart, soul, mind, and strength, and to love your neighbor as yourself (see Matthew 22:36-40). Yet we still need a day of rest. The spirit of that commandment lives on.

TED... Our family Sabbath includes parts of two days. It starts on Sunday afternoon and goes through Monday afternoon. On Sunday afternoon we feel the pressure of a week completed, and we create space between the conclusion of the week and the start of a new one. On Monday afternoon, Amy and I gear up for the upcoming work/school week.

Breaking the Sabbath is a great temptation. We are tempted every Monday to dive into work. We even have devices that allow us to take our work with us wherever we go. The other day I was looking on Facebook at some pictures that my mom took at our son's birthday party. We celebrated his birthday on our Sabbath, Monday. This is very embarrassing, but in every picture my violation was glaring. In every picture, I had my BlackBerry (or as Amy affectionately calls it, my "Crackberry") in hand. Texting and checking e-mails was my crime, evident in almost every picture. Fortunately for me, Facebook allows you to remove the tag on photos. I removed the tag on every last one of them. The link to evidence of my sin has been destroyed. Technology these days requires that you stay on your toes.

Relax Your Soul and Enjoy Quietness

Sixty-two percent of Americans in a recent survey believe that they are burned out or on the edge of burnout. Psalm 23:1-2 says, "The LORD is my shepherd, I shall not be in want. He makes me lie down in green pastures." Every time I read that, I think of the times God has made me lie down. Have you experienced those times? You ran at an unhealthy pace, then God gave you a continual Sabbath with two or three weeks in the hospital because you neglected this principle of rest.

You weren't taking care of yourself. You didn't build rest into your lifestyle, so God made you lie down.

GARY... I can act pretty tough when it comes to rest and relaxation. One thing I always share at seminars right out of the chute is "I am seventy, but I feel like I am forty." My spirit cries out forty, but my body cries out, "Slow down, Gary Smalley!" I usually like to think I can travel and speak more than my body or emotions allow. My wife and staff protect me the best they can from a frantic pace. They know that the noise, lines, and schedules of airports these days wear on my nerves. For years, God has forced me to lie down.

I often wonder if a regular Sabbath would have kept me from my heart attack and kidney transplant. I can't say for sure, but I have had a lot of family stress throughout the years of raising kids and even now as a marriage champion with three adult children desiring to be marriage champions as well. I was trying to make my kids happy and at the same time placed Norma's desires on the back burner. I am convinced that my efforts to be a great parent laid me flat on my back in the woods waiting to die.

Out of cell-phone range when turkey hunting with my friend Junior, I had a full-blown heart attack with 100 percent blockage. I remember lying on the ground, resting my head against a firm bag, and looking at the sky. I can still remember the sense of peace that came over me. I prayed, "God, I will see you in a couple of minutes. Thank you for my life and my family." I smiled at the thought of my kids and my wife. I felt like I was dying.

But I didn't die that day. That's stating the obvious. Junior carried my weak body to the truck and drove to cell phone range. The paramedics came and took me by helicopter to the nearest hospital. On the way, I had enough strength and sound mind to call my wife, who was running our ministry at the time. I said, "I Ion!"

"Hold on, I got somebody in here," she answered and put me on hold.

Even as I thought I was going to die, I was irritated. My wife had put me on hold! I told myself, *Fine, I will never talk to her again*—even though I wanted to talk to her one last time more than anything in the whole world.

When we got to the hospital, Norma was running alongside the gurney when she leaned down and spoke words I will never forget: "You listen to me. You are not dying, and you are not leaving me with this mess."

Down to the very end, my wife was trying to control me! I say that in jest, of course. But that episode was a defining moment for me. There in that hospital bed in Springfield, Missouri, I decided two things. One, I was going to place Norma above every earthly relationship I had. Two, I was going to find rest for my soul and peace from my stress. Actually, the doctor prescribed number two as well.

I usually don't ever beg my readers, but I feel the need to right here. Pleeeaaassse, grab hold of the reins of your home and pull back on them. Slow down. Relax. Enjoy your spouse. And do so before God lays you down. Enjoy the quietness without the noise of the world, without the news of the world, and just be alone. This is where I struggle with something the church calls quiet times. It feels like a waste of time. You get into it, and if you're like me, you can be praying and really there, and then go, "I need to change out the air filters in our HVAC system." I find myself journaling the size of the air filters in our home. It's hard for me to be quiet. Then I start scheduling out my workweek.

TED... Here's how it usually starts for me. On our Sabbath we spend moments throughout the day getting alone and being quiet. We try to turn the world off, but that is usually when a flood of thoughts hits us.

I sit in the living room for a few moments of quiet, and it starts. Since I just turned off my computer, my thoughts immediately go to *When did I last back up my computer? Joe never called me back.*

I replay nightmares in my head, news problems, my car's need for an oil change. *I might as well get the car inspected while the oil is changed.*

Crud, I gotta go to the license bureau. I wonder who is trying to call me right now. Does my cell need charging? Should I do my laundry today or tomorrow? Oh yes, I'm going to be still before the Lord.

Then the kids scream, "DAD!"

Okay, am I doing it right? Is it really getting me anywhere? Am I going to grow from this? God, are you really . . . ?

"DAD!"

How much longer is this going to last?

"DAD!"

I better take a look. . . . A cup of coffee would be nice right now; this one's getting a little cold. I should have had it before I started. Am I falling asleep? I feel tired. Should I go for a full day of work, or should I slack a little tomorrow? Ted, you're wasting precious time. Why does my stomach hurt? I had an uncle who died of stomach cancer. Should I eat more fiber? I know there's a new health-food store that just opened down the way; I better check that out. Should I get on freecreditreport.com and see what my credit score is doing in this economy? It doesn't really matter what your credit score is anymore because you can't get any money. I just know this time of being still and silent before God is really helping. It's clearing my mind and helping me see things a lot better. Jesus, I love you. Thank you for giving me this time with you. I better get going. I wonder how many e-mails are waiting for me once I turn this computer back on.

That's quietness for me. I don't know if it is as much about our busyness as it is about our distractions. I think *busyness* is just a nicer word, a socially acceptable word, for distracted. We often fail to live a centered life and a life oriented around God, as if God is merely along for the ride most of the time.

Psalm 23:3 goes on to say, "He restores my soul." I have to remain connected to the Source, and the only way I can do that is by slowing myself down long enough and being quiet long enough to hear from him.

♥

"The apostles gathered around Jesus and reported to him all they had done and taught" (Mark 6:30). They were running full steam in their ministry, giving the reports to him. "Then, because so many people were coming and going that they did not even have a chance to eat, he said to them, 'Come with me by yourselves to a quiet place and get some rest'" (Mark 6:31). With all wisdom, Jesus knew they needed to rest and refuel to avoid burnout.

There is never going to be a shortage of ministry. There is never going to be a shortage of opportunity for you to work your job. There will always be something left to do after you leave. Often one of the hardest things to do is leave the task and pick it up when you get back.

Jesus valued rest. Why? Because his Father valued rest. Nobody is responsible for your emotional gauge other than you. "What good is it for a man to gain the whole world, yet forfeit his soul?" (Mark 8:36). What good is it? What good is it for us to run crazy, chasing the American dream, trying to make a ton of money and forget the spiritual aspect of rest, reconnecting with God, being recharged and refueled? Need more convincing? Jesus went on to say, "What can a man give in exchange for his soul?" (verse 37).

What are you exchanging for your soul? Dad or husband, Mom or wife, what are you giving up to maintain the lifestyle you've created for your family? What are you giving up by chasing your career or your dream? What are you giving up by not giving some of your downtime, your rest time, to your family?

Focus on Each Other

As parents, we can show our love by scheduling special times with the family. Communicating warm, loving approval to our children doesn't just happen naturally.

Schedule times on your Sabbath that are meaningful for all persons involved. The activity itself is not so important, but it needs to be something that is enjoyable for both the child and the parent. Often the deepest relationships can be developed during the simplest activities.

A study of 1,500 households by the University of Michigan found mothers working outside the home spend an average of eleven minutes a day on weekdays and thirty minutes a day on weekends with the children (not including mealtime). Fathers spend an average of eight minutes a day on weekdays and fourteen minutes a day on weekends in different activities with their children. At first glance, it appears that study flies in the face of the premise of this book because it doesn't sound like much time focusing on the kids. But it shows that we may be together, but not intentionally together. We may be in the same house, but in different rooms. We may be in the same room, but disconnected. This disconnection is a result of marginless living and leads to greater guilt and permissive parenting. Margin connects us and focuses our time on each other.

TED… I love when a hectic mom or dad tells me, "Ted, it is not the quantity of time, it is the quality of time." Ha! That's a good one. Spoken straight from the mouth of someone without margin.

Jerry Jenkins gets a little more to the point when he says, "I learned the idea of Quality Time was an evil lie. Some experts pushed the idea that successful overachievers, those we call Yuppies today, could have children and be guilt-free about the little time they were able to devote to them. The remedy was Quality Time. Sort of like one-minute parenting. It went like this: Be sure to make what little time you are able to spend with your child Quality Time. What garbage. I've seen the results of kids who were given only Quality Time. The problem is that kids don't know the difference. What they need is time—all they can get. Quantity time is quality time, whether you're discussing the meaning of the cosmos or just climbing on Dad."[1]

GARY… When our kids were little, I started speaking at family retreats and conferences across the country. As I spoke, I'd pick out families who looked happy and seemed to respond well to each other. When I had the opportunity, I'd approach the husband and wife with several questions.

First, I'd ask, "You seem to enjoy each other so much and have a real love for one another! What do you think is the most important thing you do as a family that makes you so close?"

Almost without exception, each family I interviewed said, "We've made a commitment to spend quality and quantity time together regularly. We have separate interests, but we make sure we do things together as a family on a regular basis."

Then I'd ask, "What's the one thing you do more than any other that you feel bonds you together?" Time and time again, I'd hear an answer that I simply couldn't believe. What was the common denominator of almost every one of these "successful" families? Camping!

At that time, Norma and I had never camped together—by choice. But since learning this secret, we camped together frequently for more than fifteen years while our children were younger. We spent many a Sabbath at campgrounds. That gives me some authority to speak on the subject, and I can say with absolute conviction—camping is not the secret. Before I let our noncamping friends off the hook, though, I do need to say that camping is still the best method I know to find the real secret to a close-knit family. The secret is spending quality and quantity time together.

When the Sabbath commandment was given, what were the children of Israel doing? Camping! Interesting, huh? Didn't know at the time I was being so literal with the text.

Add your voice to the GPLL message . . .

Connect with us at www.greatparentslousylovers.com and watch the video podcast for chapter 7.

Post your thoughts, comments, and stories on our Web site. Here are some questions from chapter 7 to get you started on your journey to a couple-centered home:

- What are the wake-up calls or warning signs for you that your margin has filled up?
- What day of the week makes the most sense for your Sabbath? Why?
- How will you turn your day off into a day of rest?
- What activities do you label as quality time?
- To what activities can you give a little more quantity time?

TIME-OUT DATE:

You've likely wanted to ask for one on occasion since the kids arrived, but you're typically the ones doling them out . . . the infamous *time-out*. Well, you need one, and so does your spouse. Do not argue with us, or you'll get more time added. Spend time praying together, resting together, romancing together.

CHAPTER 8

FOUR SPIRITUAL JOURNEYS

You might be a Great Parent, Lousy Lover if you have adult
children living at home and they refuse to give up their Star
Wars bedsheets.

TED... Bedtime is our best part of the day. Gary challenged
us a long time ago to start asking Corynn and Carson this
question every night: "What are the three most important
things in life?"

Corynn is the first to respond with "Honor God, honor
others, and honor God's creation."

"That's right," Amy and I respond in unison.

But then Corynn usually has a follow-up question: "Dad,
who do you love more, me or Mom?" Ouch! My first response
is usually to act like I didn't hear the question, or I squint
my eyes as though I did not understand the question. If that
doesn't work, I change the subject. With her short attention

span, I sometimes get lucky. But more often than not, she persists.

"I love your mommy and you both," I say gently, "but God wants me to love Mommy in a different way. Your mommy is stuck with me for life. We are going to kiss and hug and love all over each other until one of us goes to heaven or Jesus returns. But you, Corynn, will not be with us forever. You will one day leave our home and start one of your own."

After she "ews" and "ughs" over the kissing and hugging part, Corynn is quick to reply, "I want to be with you and Mommy forever."

"You can't be with us forever, Corynn," I insist.

As tears form in her eyes, she glares at me and says, "I am going to college online and staying home forever." While I like the sound of that from a tuition standpoint, I need her to know that separation from Mom and Dad is a sign of health and maturity. She will need to leave home one day.

Of course, part of me wants her to stay home. But I have been handed the assignment to start her on her spiritual journey for life. I won't be with her for three-quarters of her life, but God has given me this time on the front end to invest in her and to help form the beliefs of her heart.

———— 💔 ————

Most people point to Genesis 2:24 as a marriage verse, but it first serves as a verse to instruct parents on how to order the spiritual journeys in the home. The "leave and cleave" texts of the Bible are most often taught to adults. "For this reason a man will leave his father and mother and be united to his wife, and they will become one flesh" (Genesis 2:24). The King James Version uses the word *cleave* to convey being united. These words, first given in the Garden of Eden, were given to a couple who had no biological parents. One must wonder if God was instructing Adam and Eve on how they were to raise their children, rather than giving them a teaching for future marriages. This teaching would first be given to children, not adults. We have no record of the talk, but I wonder when Adam and Eve first taught Genesis 2:24 to Cain and Abel.

While weddings are the primary venue for this "leave and cleave" teaching, we can't delay teaching our kids the importance of leaving home. Bedtime prayers with your kindergartner present the perfect teachable moment. My children and yours need to learn the core value of maturity at an early age. Maturity defined for our children is simply "understanding that you will not be with your mom and dad forever and planning accordingly."

Jay Adams writes, "God did not put a parent and child into the garden. Adam and Eve were husband and wife. . . . The relationship between parent and child is established through birth (or adoption); the relationship between husband and wife by covenant promises. Blood may be thicker than water, but it should not be thicker than promise. The contrast between the temporary parent-child relationship and the permanent husband-wife relationship once again forcefully points up the uniqueness of marriage in God's plan for human beings."

Marriage involves a new priority. When you see the word *leave* you may think you need to move a thousand miles away from Mom and Dad. The focus of this text is not geographical. Most young couples live in close proximity to their parents and move away later. The focus of this text is relational. The husband-wife bond is to be stronger than the parent-child bond.

Understanding the significance of "leaving and cleaving" is one of the most important things you can do for your family, not just your marriage. In this one passage (Genesis 2:24), four spiritual journeys are at play: husband, wife, marriage, and child. Let's explore the significance of the "leaving."

"Leaving" is the idea that no relationship, apart from your relationship with God, is more important than your marriage. To leave means to forsake, depart from, leave behind, and abandon. Your marriage was the first relationship that started your family. You had to leave your parents to get married.

Your journey and your spouse's journey combined to form a third journey—your marriage. When you delivered your first child, a fourth journey entered your home, and the "leave" cycle started all over again.

FOUR SPIRITUAL JOURNEYS

TED... From the moment your child is born, you are entrusted to raise that child in the Lord to ultimately leave home and make wise adult decisions. It is a hard truth to fathom when you are swaddling a baby dependent on your constant oversight and support. The work that goes into the early years forms a bond that is tight. I never truly understood this bond until Amy and I visited the doctor's office in the fall of 2003.

As Amy mentioned already, the first several weeks of breastfeeding did not go well. Each feeding lasted an hour, but Corynn was still hungry at the end. It was a very emotional time. Amy would nurse every other hour for an hour, and we knew it was not enough. There were many tears all around.

At our regularly scheduled doctor's appointment, they did the usual routine: measured, weighed, and prodded. When the doctor came in and the charts popped up on the office PC, he said rather flippantly, "Well, looks like she ain't getting enough to eat." Feeling helpless and disconnected, Amy lost it. The tears flowed again.

At that moment I finally got it. I finally understood the bond that exists between Mom and baby. It is actually the same bond that God uses as a word picture to describe his connection to his children: "Can a mother forget the baby at her breast and have no compassion on the child she has borne?" (Isaiah 49:15). I have seen the sadness in a mother's eyes when she no longer is able to nurse her child.

We have a sweet lady in our church with eight children. She nursed each child for the first eighteen months of life. Let me do the math for you. She spent twelve years of her life nursing children. When they lost their ninth child during pregnancy, I remember her telling me, "Ted, the thing I will miss the most is that bond that forms during nursing."

I now get it.

With my understanding of a mother's bond, and as a loving father, I know that this idea of our kids leaving home is a tough truth. As strong as that bond is, and though it is a bond created by almighty God, it is not meant to have the permanence of marriage. God never calls you as a parent to cleave to your children. The word *cleave* in the Hebrew literally reads "and he shall cling to his wife." The sooner I grasp this distinction as a parent, the sooner I embrace the true purpose of parenting. Throughout life, our attachments and loyalties to our parents go very deep, affecting us long after we leave home, and even long after they pass away. But in a nutshell, you cling to your spouse, not to your children.

Many parents of adult children never truly allow those children to "leave" home, and they cling to them as adults. I call this the "Barone syndrome." The hit television show *Everybody Loves Raymond* gives us a clear example of parents who are way too involved in the lives of their children and grandchildren. Grandma and Grandpa serve as a safety net for tough times, as babysitters, and will even offer unsolicited advice when they see problems in the marriage. I know we said earlier that the "leave" text does not refer to geography, but if you live near your parents and you sense the Barone syndrome, run as fast and as far away as you can!

———————— 💜 ————————

There are three key reasons for adopting a "leave and cleave" parenting style.

First, it starts children on their spiritual journey and prepares them for adulthood. Adulthood defined is taking personal responsibility for your thoughts, emotions, actions, and reactions. Teaching your children that they will not be with you forever and to plan accordingly begins them on the journey toward becoming adults.

We believe that many parents today are delaying their children's spiritual journeys and that prolonged adolescence is preventing kids from growing up. We are teaching our kids how to be dependent on us rather than how to live independent of us. Invented in 1904, the term *adolescence* stems from the Latin, *adolescere*, meaning "to grow up."[1] This man-made age is a period of time when a person is no longer a child but not yet an adult. From the time God breathed Genesis 2:24 and through the first several thousand years of human history, kids became adults. It has only been in the past one hundred–plus years that kids have been delayed from growing up. We have inserted this ten- to fifteen-year stretch between childhood and adulthood. The Bible only uses the terms *child* and *adult*. There was no gap between the two. Children became adults. While Scripture gives many responsibilities to parents, the apostle Paul sums it up with this command: "Fathers, do not exasperate your children; instead, bring them up in the training and instruction of the Lord" (Ephesians 6:4). Our job as parents is to instruct our children so that, when they become adults, they have a love for the Lord and the things that please God.

TED... As a senior pastor, I have hired many college graduates to serve in the church. Every single hire has frustrated me considerably. I used to think these twentysomethings were lazy and disrespectful of authority. But I have come to learn that I am the first person in their lives to challenge them out of adolescence and into adulthood. Part of being an adult is leaving home, making wise adult decisions, and taking responsibility for the outcome. Most parents today are controllers of their teens' behavior rather than monitors. Don't wait too long to teach your kids to be adults. Children need to be taught independence, not dependence.

———— 💜 ————

Second, the "leave and cleave" parenting style guards parents from becoming overprotective. Hovering parents communicate through word and deed that their children cannot be trusted. Understanding the parenting implications of the "leave and cleave" texts continually reminds us that our children need to take chances, make mistakes, learn, and go on. As parents we become monitors of their progress rather than just controllers of their behavior.

Later in life, difficulties arise when parents try to control and manipulate their adult children after they are married. Often parents are simply trying to get their own needs for love met. Parents can actually rob the lives of their children to fulfill their own selfish desires.

Understanding the "leave and cleave" parenting style guards against becoming an overprotective, dominant, and controlling parent.

Third, the "leave and cleave" parenting style establishes order in the home. This parenting style constantly keeps in front of the kids that they are a welcomed addition to the family and that they won't be here forever. It reminds them that Mom and Dad will stay married and enjoy life long after they are gone. How many times do we see families where the kids operate with an attitude that says, "What in the world will Mom and Dad do with their time once I'm gone?" After all, the school years were spent with Mom and Dad attending games, carpooling, and paying for cell phones. What will their purpose in life be during the empty-nesting years? We ask that question tongue in cheek.

TED... I want my children to learn maturity at an early age. Again, we define maturity in our home as "knowing I will not be with Mom and Dad forever and planning accordingly." Separation from parents is good and healthy. Good parenting recognizes the blessing that every child needs to one day be released to a new journey with Christ and his or her mate. Our children need to be instilled with confidence that they will one day make capable, adult decisions on their own.

I talk to adult children all the time who are still calling home in their twenties and thirties asking for money. Then they get frustrated over how their parents are so controlling. Hello! I first tell them to get the Star Wars bedsheets off the bed. Then they must grow up.

When I am doing premarital counseling, I make sure young couples get this. The conversation usually goes something like this: "Before you call home asking for money, think through the interest payments. You have no idea how much it will cost you to borrow two hundred dollars. You will pay on it for years. You will pay with the interest of lack of trust, controlling maneuvers, and occasional guilt trips."

Also, age does not determine adulthood. Sure eighteen is the legal age, but I know very few eighteen-year-old adults. Adulthood defined means making adult decisions on your own. It is about taking personal responsibility for your actions, words, reactions, and decisions. It's about making right decisions even when you are not being watched.

Proverbs 23:22-25 says, "Listen to your father, who gave you life, and do not despise your mother when she is old.

Buy the truth and do not sell it; get wisdom, discipline and understanding. The father of a righteous man has great joy; he who has a wise son delights in him. May your father and mother be glad." As parents we want to delight in our children. We want to know that our journey has rubbed off on them. I want to look at Carson and say, "You are my son, and I am well pleased."

Great parenting is all about strategic separation. Adult decisions require a healthy separation from Mom and Dad. Knowing that you have raised your kids to make adult decisions brings delight to you as their parent.

Amy and I have a plan to give distance to our children as they grow. This separation is not about keeping our kids from making bad decisions, but directing them toward good ones. And separation is part of the directing. Separation says, "I will not always be with you when you need to make life decisions, so I will back away and allow you to make the call."

Proverbs 23:25 goes on to say, "May she who gave you birth rejoice!" As parents we rejoice when our kids begin acting like responsible adults. Isn't that the goal of parenting?

My parents had a "leave and cleave" parenting style and were definitely not the hovering kind. They understood the four spiritual journeys and constantly taught toward that end.

Here's the thing about my mom that I love more than anything: When I was growing up, my mom, before leaving the house each morning, would stand at the bottom of the stairs and shout up at me, "Don't let the turkeys get you down." She even bought a shirt one time with those words on the front. I was a little, chubby kid and had some problems at school. She knew I would be on my own there. Rather than shelter me, she sent me into the world with her turkey theology.

My mom always told me to go for it. She wrote me a letter when I was four years old in which she released me to the Lord. It said, "Lord, wherever he goes, use him for your Kingdom. If you send him to Africa, Asia, or a remote island, please use him. I am not going to hold him back. God, he is yours; I have him for a short time." Some thirty years later I still remember those words. She knew who I belonged to.

My dad started early with the "leave and cleave" parenting style. I'll never forget that every Sunday morning, like clockwork, he called his mom and dad to check on them. He also sent his parents money every month. My dad taught me a strong work ethic. He had me earning money by the age of seven. Never once did the police knock on our door for child-labor law violations. If I wanted something special, he would sit down with me and help me develop a plan to earn it.

He was a giving guy, but he didn't give me everything for free. If I had to get the car fixed, he kept a ledger, and I paid him back. Again, what a cruel dad! He would give me an allowance, after I worked for it, then he would sit me down and say, "Here's the money going to savings, here's the money going to the church, and here's spending money." I still tithe today because I picture my dad sitting down with a few bucks of my allowance showing me how to divide my money. He taught me how to be a giver. My mom and dad allowed me, from a very early age, to make adult decisions. They gave me a lot of freedom to do that.

My parents enjoy being empty nesters. At first I didn't know how to feel about that. My mom turned my childhood bedroom into a reading room shortly after I left home. They didn't even ask! The nerve! Over the years I have received phone calls from my parents saying, "We found another box of your precious childhood memories. Do you want us to send it to you, or can we pitch it?" My parents have a great sense of humor. But this I know, they have definitely released me. I've been gone from home going on twenty years now, and I am thrilled to report that I have never once asked for money from my parents. And trust me, they are equally as thrilled.

Have you released your kids to the Lord? Do you promote the four spiritual journeys in your home? I love when we do baby dedications at Woodland Hills Family Church. They serve as a reminder to us that the children do not belong to us, but rather they have been entrusted to us to care for, teach, train, and send.

While researching for this book, I put a wall post on Facebook asking my friends to share their struggles of being great parents and lousy lovers. To remain anonymous, most did not respond on my wall, but I did receive a ton of messages. The following Facebook message is a good representation of the whole:

"I must admit that my husband and I attended your

conference in San Antonio, Texas. We tried lighting the candle to prepare each other for the night of lovemaking, but for some reason that fell by the wayside. As a family (two little girls) we are awesome, we love each other, but when it comes to US we are just not there. We have been married for twelve years. I am back in college full-time trying to finish up my degree. He works nights, and I hope that when I finish school he will be able to quit his job and take a little break. I am soooo sorry for our love life that we make no time for it because we are so occupied with making sure that we have a future for our girls. So to sum it all up, I would say that we are trying to be Great Parents and are truly Lousy Lovers."

———————— 💔 ————————

Mom and Dad, there are three journeys you must care for before your child's.

You must take 100 percent responsibility for your own spiritual journey. You must spend regular time in God's Word and on your knees with your heavenly Father.

You must assist your spouse's spiritual journey while removing all expectations for him or her to meet your spiritual and emotional needs.

You must care for and invest in your marriage journey. Staying married for life is not enough. You must begin again learning how to enjoy life with each other (see Ecclesiastes 9:9).

Then, and only then, will you have something to give your children. It starts with you.

Add your voice to the GPLL message . . .

Connect with us at www.greatparentslousylovers.com and watch the video podcast for chapter 8.

Post your thoughts, comments, and stories on our Web site. Here are some questions from chapter 8 to get you started on your journey to a couple-centered home:

- Have you left home emotionally, relationally, and financially?
- If yes, what are you doing to make sure your children do the same?
- Why do you think Genesis 2:24 is more of a parenting verse, rather than a marriage verse?
- At what age do you think it is best to start teaching your kids that they will not be with Mom and Dad forever and they need to start planning accordingly? Why?
- Name a few boundaries that parents need to create with their adult children.

JOURNAL-THE-JOURNEY DATE:

Whether or not you plan to renew your vows officially, spend time rewriting your promises to each other now. With the life and parenting experience you've gained since you became husband and wife, what would you include in your updated vows? What do you love about your mate even more now than when you said, "I do"? Read your renewed promises to each other, and put them where you'll be reminded of the love and life you share.

CHAPTER 9

YOUR SPIRITUAL JOURNEY

You might be a Great Parent, Lousy Lover if your only alone time with God is to calm you down and to keep you from "going off" on someone small.

GARY... The best gift I can give Norma and my kids is a home where they can be honored. I begin wrapping this gift when I stop working on them and start working on myself. Galatians 6:5 says, "We are each responsible for our own conduct" (NLT). I can only work on myself and change me. Working on my heart and my beliefs is the first and foremost spiritual journey.

———— ♥ ————

Proverbs 4:23 says, "Above all else, guard your heart, for it is the wellspring of life." Stand watch over your heart. Take a good, close look. Look at what is going on in there, and realize that what is happening in your life and in your conflict is coming from your heart, not your mate, children, or circumstances.

Matthew 12:34 says, "Out of the overflow of the heart the mouth speaks." The heart determines my actions and my reactions. What is coming out of my mouth or the way in which I act out is the result of the heart.

We love the illustration Andy Stanley, senior pastor of Northpoint Community Church near Atlanta, Georgia, uses to describe the condition of the heart in marriage. Picture two jars: one filled with blue jelly beans and one filled with pink jelly beans. When you bump the two jars into each other, the blue beans fall out of the blue jar, and the pink beans fall out of the pink jar. Our first reaction is to fault the other person for what fell out of the jar. "Look what you did!" we say. But in reality, our spouse isn't responsible for what comes out. Yes, he or she might have triggered it, but the jelly beans were there all along.

In marriage, when your spouse "bumps" you, stuff begins to spill out of you. What spills out of you was already in there. Your spouse did not put it there. He or she helped bring it to the surface. A goal of a healthy marriage is not to keep from bumping each other, but rather to own what comes out. This is the emphasis of Proverbs 27:19: "As water reflects a face, so a man's heart reflects the man" and Proverbs 23:7: "For as he thinks in his heart, so is he" (NKJV). Everything we see about you on the outside is just a reflection of what is going on in your heart.

Jesus taught the exact same thing when his disciples were chastised for not ceremonially cleansing their hands before they ate. Matthew 15:16-20 shares the story: "'Don't you understand yet?' Jesus asked. 'Anything you eat passes through the stomach and then goes into the sewer. But the words you speak come from the heart—that's what defiles you. For from the heart come evil thoughts, murder, adultery, all sexual immorality, theft, lying, and slander. These are what defile you'" (NLT). Evil comes from within, not without.

When I focus on my mate's behavior rather than mine, I waste precious time that could have been spent on my spiritual journey. Not only do we hide behind our spouse's spiritual journey, but we like to hide behind our marriage journey as well.

TED... Fred and Cheryl were hiding behind each other and their marriage. Separated after fifteen years of marriage, Cheryl was done playing the games. I have counseled many couples out of extramarital affairs, but I had never seen anything like the pit this couple lived in. These two used affairs to get even with each other. By the time they walked through the doors of Woodland Hills, Fred had been with eight different women in those fifteen years, and Cheryl had been with six different guys. It was retaliatory sex. This was the first couple I had ever met who truly hated each other. It was also the first time I used Jesus' "love your enemies" command in marriage counseling (see Matthew 5:44; Luke 6:27, 35).

Where do you start with a couple this angry? I began with an observation.

"Fred. Cheryl. It's obvious that you two hate each other. And it's apparent that you don't have a marriage here. I rarely, if ever, counsel divorce, but in this case I must in order to prevent a murder—but I need to ask you a question. Do I have your permission to ask you a spiritual question?"

"I guess," Fred mumbled.

"What if I told you both that you do not have a marital problem?" I asked.

"Huh?" Cheryl asked in surprise.

"Marriage and sex are not the problems here," I continued. "What's going on in your marriage, and in your bed, well, those are just symptoms of a greater need."

"Jesus, right?" Fred asked reluctantly. After all, they were in a pastor's office.

"Fred, all of your anger, rage, and discontentment stem from the lack of fulfillment in your life," I said. "You must resolve your anger with the only true Source of life."

Fred, Cheryl, and I met more than a dozen times after that first session. That was just the beginning of their new life in Christ. I encouraged them with a key to understanding spiritual growth: Take responsibility for your own—and only your own—spiritual journey. You must identify your own need for Christ to fill the emptiness in your life. This first step begins a journey, not a race. Too often we like to package life change in a nice and neat six- or thirteen-week Bible study. This misconception has created a faulty idea that life change happens fast. I believe real life change is typically slow. I like to think in terms of years, not weeks or months. This alone should encourage a couple not to think their marriage will be perfect or on track after a few sessions with a pastor or counselor. Give it time. Fred and Cheryl spent more than a dozen weeks just taking the first step: taking 100 percent personal responsibility for their separate spiritual journeys.

When I perform marriage ceremonies and a couple wants to use a unity candle as a part of the service, I no longer have the couple blow out the two candles once they light the middle one. Instead, I have them keep their individual candles lit. I understand the imagery behind oneness as part of the tradition. However, taken to the extreme, this leads to codependence. There are three journeys at the wedding: your journey, your mate's journey, and the marital journey. Three lit candles best represent the truth that a marriage relationship is between the husband, the wife, and God.

As we pursue God together, the distance between us grows smaller. If you are a follower of Jesus Christ—meaning you believe that he has been raised from the dead and you are a saved person by confessing him as Lord and Boss of your life, and you are growing in the faith—you have the Spirit of God living within you.

GARY... As a seventy-year-old man I have learned from my own studies over the last ten years this great truth that I must work on myself first and foremost. I may be seventy, but I feel forty because God's power is more alive in me today than ever before. I jump out of bed every morning to take personal responsibility for my heart and my beliefs. Allow me to share with you the top four beliefs for your spiritual journey. Here is how I guard my heart, the wellspring of life.

1. I humble myself before God and my family.

Since as humans, we are incapable of creating or manufacturing anything close to the love, power, and fulfillment God offers us, we are humble and helpless, like beggars crying out to God. As a result of this "poor in Spirit" position, he gives us his grace, love, power, and high quality of life. After we humble ourselves before God and our family, we gain his love and power.

As we continue to admit that we don't have God's love or power within our natural human selves, he gives us all the tools and abilities we would ever need to become like him— holy! We are "twigs" unable to produce his "fruit" hanging upon us. We are helpless unless God "grafts" us into his Vine, Jesus Christ (see John 15:1-12).

God nurtures us until he sees his "Fruit of the Spirit" begin to grow within us (see Galatians 5:22-23). At first our love is only a small, green lump reflected in our behavior. But in time, each "lump" will continue to grow until it becomes a fully ripened, purple, "loving" grape. It becomes delicious to the taste of all who are in contact with us. We become the sweet taste of Christ, but only if we remain helpless beggars. If we try to produce the grapes on our own, we can destroy them in our life. And we would become boastful and prideful if we could produce our own fruit. Just a reminder: God resists the proud (see 1 Peter 5:5). We don't want to take credit for any of the qualities God produces within us.

Humility is a lost virtue in most homes today. Marriages and families must start with James 4:6: "God opposes the proud but gives grace to the humble."

2. I commit to love God with all my heart, soul, mind, and strength.

This is the greatest commandment (see Mark 12:29-30). I want it to be true of me. But with any relationship, I cannot fall in love with someone I do not know. I also cannot commit to love him until I am humbled, realizing how dead I am without him.

Ted and I have two dear friends in Franklin, Tennessee, who challenge us more than anyone to care for our personal spiritual journey. Phil and Heather Joel have seen success, worked at a pace that outran their souls, and sacrificed much over the years for their careers. But they had a wake-up call that changed all of that. They speak of their need to reconnect with the Source and spend time every day getting to know the Lord. Their Web site, www.deliberatepeople.com, tells their story:

> It's simple. The idea of daily getting away to be alone with God and learning to hear His voice through reading the Bible and prayer is not exactly an

original thought, but it is one that we believe God wants us to get back to in these crazy days.

Coming to Him, seeking Him, pursuing Him, drawing near to Him . . . however you want to say it, it's all about a relationship with our Creator. He has ideas, dreams and plans for our lives and promises to show them to us as we take time to be still and ask Him to speak to us . . . positioning ourselves every day to hear from Him and to communicate with Him. In essence, building a relationship.

Today, the culture we live in is in direct opposition to this. This is the age where faster is better. With the emergence of social network websites and instant everything, our communication, although at an all time high in regard to quantity, is heading to an all time low in quality. We collect friends with the click of a mouse and the art of true relationship through real communication and time is fast becoming a thing of the past.

This "advancement" in culture has moved its way into the fabric of our homes and churches. The good old saying "Christianity is not a religion but a relationship" has become an old fashioned phrase for "idealistic, out of touch" people who "need to get out more."

Eight years ago, Heather and I had an awakening—a realization. We became frightfully aware that we knew a lot about the Lord but, if we were honest, we didn't really know Him. We'd been moving so fast in life that our pursuit of Him was reduced to church on Sunday, prayer before meals, and the odd Oswald Chambers devotional. One-on-one time alone with Him wasn't a part of our day, and prayer time didn't exist—we knew there had to be more. Not long after, someone gave us a one-year Bible reading schedule that served as a tool to help us get into the Word and become more deliberate in building our relationship with Him. In years past we would have scoffed at the thought of getting up every day to be with God, but once we made it a part of our lives, God's presence and reality started to change us. He began to speak to us and show us things that only He could.

We came to see that as we pursue the reality of God in our lives we begin learning to hear His voice in this noisy world, we find our purpose in life—and that purpose is to be in a loving relationship with Him and with people. Without loving and enjoying God first, we don't have anything of real value to pass on to our spouse, kids, friends, and world.

Your spiritual journey is more important than packing lunches, changing the channel from Disney to the Cartoon Network, and building a retirement fund. Why? Because you cannot give what you do not have. You and I do not produce or generate one ounce of love. "We love because he first loved us" (1 John 4:19). It is only after I fill myself with God's love that I have something to give my spouse, children, and grandchildren.

He meets all your needs through Christ Jesus. There are no more expectations on anyone or anything else to give you what you need or desire. He gives it all. No more stress from expectations you create on this earth because all of your expectations are now from him. It's comforting to know that he knows exactly what you need and when you really need to receive it.

3. I work every day to love my spouse as myself.

After humbling yourself, you will have both the desire and ability from his gift of love and power to "love your neighbor as yourself" (Matthew 19:19, NLT). It will become easier for you to love your neighbors in the same way that you enjoy being loved, respected, forgiven, and treated with tenderness and acts of kindness. Your strong desire to love and care for mankind comes from God, who is now filling you up with the fullness of himself. Loving your neighbors will become a natural, eager desire.

He is the giver of the fullest life on this earth and forevermore into eternity. He meets all your needs through his riches in Christ Jesus (see Philippians 4:19), so you can take your eyes off your own needs, knowing that God watches over you as a loving Father and cares for you every day, all day. That's peace you can't get from anywhere else! It's just another awesome truth for you while you wait for and trust him to direct your paths.

A number of years ago I returned from a two-week conference where I learned about the value of honoring others. I realized that I had been expecting Norma to "make me happy" in the sexual area. At this conference, I learned a life-changing principle: When we give up our life for others, we gain it back from God.

I went home not knowing what to expect. All I wanted to do was serve my wife because God was filling me up with himself. After three weeks, Norma asked me why I hadn't pursued sex. I surprised myself—I hadn't even thought of it! I was focusing on serving God and giving him a chance to meet all of my needs, and he was faithfully doing it.

I explained to her that I didn't want to place any expectations on her but just serve her the best I could. Then she said something I'll never forget: "I need it, too, you know. I need to be held, and I enjoy it too."

I had never heard those words before. When you dedicate yourself to serving, valuing, and honoring your spouse, he or she will start looking for ways to love you back. My wife never resisted sex again.

4. I give God thanks in and for ALL circumstances.

I can give personal testimony today that God has turned everything negative that has happened to me into something good. Could it be that the apostle Paul boasted about all of his difficulties and trials because each one of those hard times brought him more of God's patience and many other of God's qualities? (See Romans 5:3-5.) He held on to God's hope and was never disappointed. Through those hardships, God's love continued to flow into his heart from the Holy Spirit.

As you and I continue to humble ourselves, God's power and love help us to experience everything that happens as varying degrees of *good* or *great*. Life is full of trials and difficulties that bring us unexpected gems of good or great blessings.

One of the most awesome side effects of this fourth belief is that God promises to turn ALL of our hardships and difficulties into more of his love and power flowing into us (see 2 Corinthians 12:9-10; Romans 5:3-5). God knows and allows only things that are good for us, even if we consider them negative. You can boast about your hardship "gifts" from God because all good things come from him. As life throws you anything negative, you can expect everything to turn into good or great.

I'll rejoice in everything that happens to me. Since everything works together for my good because I love God and I've been empowered to love others—his life purpose for me—nothing is wasted. I'm never a victim. I can give thanks for all things for this is God's will through Christ Jesus. (Important note: I have discovered that we don't have to feel thankful in order to thank God. The feelings of thankfulness will follow in time after we see the good evidence from the difficulties. He's not asking us to feel thankful, but to give thanks because we believe that God is faithful. His Word is truth. He will turn our negative circumstances into something positive.)

I'm crucified with Christ, but I now live by the faith and hope of Christ who loves me and actually laid down his life for me (see Galatians 2:20)! So I constantly seek to know what "faith" he has given me in order to watch his purposes for me unfold each day of the year.

As I stated earlier, I'm seventy years old and more excited about today and what the future brings than at any other time. My life is just starting because every day is the first day of the rest of my life. I live with great hope about today and tomorrow. What will he inspire me to do today? Help someone I don't even know? Grant forgiveness to someone? Use me to bring others to him? How will he use me tomorrow? Even the littlest things I do can be used mightily by God. All things are possible through him (see Matthew 19:26). I get to discover his dreams for me and what he wants to do through me.

Nothing has changed my life more than these four beliefs. I review them each day. My friends and family are finding that I complain less and serve more. I take no credit. It is the power of God working through my spiritual journey. I find that I am overflowing each day and want to give more and more to Norma on her spiritual journey. After all, I cannot give what I do not have.

Add your voice to the GPLL message . . .

Connect with us at www.greatparentslousylovers.com and watch the video podcast for chapter 9.

Post your thoughts, comments, and stories on our Web site. Here are some questions from chapter 9 to get you started on your journey to a couple-centered home:

- When your spouse or kids "bump" you, what has been spilling out lately?
- How are you taking personal responsibility for your own spiritual journey? Who have you been blaming?
- What trials are you going through right now that you are complaining about?
- How can you turn those trials over to God and be thankful?
- Which spiritual disciplines (prayer, fasting, Bible reading, and fellowship) have you been neglecting for the kids and your spouse?
- What is your plan to care for your soul?

ROOM-TO-GROW DATE:

What character quality do you sense God working to grow in you? How will growth in this area bless your marriage? Write this quality on an index card and place it where you'll see it every day. Then take your spouse out for a quiet meal and share with him or her your commitment to pray for God's help in growing that character trait in you over the next year.

Note: Good news—this is actually two dates when both of you share.

CHAPTER 10

YOUR SPOUSE'S SPIRITUAL JOURNEY

You might be a Great Parent, Lousy Lover if you think that you don't even need a spouse to have a great marriage.

TED... Growing up independent, fundamental Baptist, I never in a million years thought I would marry someone from an Assemblies of God church. The primary difference between the two denominations can be summed up in the opposite way Amy and I interpret street signs. I view all road signs as law, and if you break them, God is going to get you. My wife, much like my coauthor, views them as suggestions for other people.

My upbringing gave me a guilt-prone nature. A while back, Amy and I went to a theme park with the kids. We brought our humongous double stroller along, and shortly after arriving at the park, our son fell asleep in it. With Carson fast asleep, we headed to the Princess Fair area. As we got to the entrance of the area, we were greeted by a large, white sign with bold, black letters that read, "No Strollers Beyond This Point." I knew as soon as we saw it that my sweet bride would interpret the sign for me. We didn't need interpreters in the Baptist church, but that was something AG churches had.

I came to a screeching halt a safe distance from the sign. Amy kept walking as though she didn't see it. I must give her the benefit of the doubt because she has conditioned herself not to see such restrictive signs. You've heard of color blindness? My wife has sign blindness.

"Carson and I are staying out here with the other hundred-plus strollers," I demanded.

Amy egged me on.

"Do you really think that sign is for everybody but you?" I asked.

She kept urging me to come in. And yes, she started to interpret. "Ted, they understand if the baby falls asleep in the stroller, and they understand that you can't leave your baby out in the stroller when you go on a ride or do an activity. Of course you can come in."

"I agree. I do not think they want you to leave the baby in the stroller parking area. But I am wondering if maybe they want you to stay with your baby," I retorted.

With that, Amy headed with Corynn to the craft tables. As they were coloring their princess tiaras, Amy peeped up over the wall to see me doing laps with Carson in the stroller parking lot. She motioned to me and called out, "Come in, there's nobody here."

I shook my head.

She motioned again and with a raspy distant voice said, "Come in here, you big baby."

Peer pressure in marriage—I give in to it every time. There was Pastor Ted looking around as I sneaked in. I hightailed it to the table and put the parking brake on the stroller. I was down there not even thirty seconds when one of Snow White's dwarfs, who had been given way too much authority for a sixteen-year-old, walked right up to me.

"Sir, strollers are not allowed in this area," he said.

My guilt-prone response was clear: "I know!"

You know what my precious wife does in situations like that? She disowns me. She doesn't make eye contact with me or with the person confronting me.

So there I stood with Dopey right in my face asking, "Sir, did you see the sign?"

"Yes, I saw the sign," I replied. I looked over to Amy for some backup, but she continued to ignore me.

"Sir, I'm going to need you to go up to stroller parking," he said as though I did not hear him the first time. Now I had offended Dopey.

A while later Amy came walking up to me where I sat sulking in stroller parking and said, "Oh, you big baby."

"Big baby? We broke a rule! The rule said no strollers! By the way, we signed a covenant. We are bonded for life, and you disowned me down there!"

That day Amy was not out to get me to break a rule or to just leave me high and dry and then laugh at my guilt. She saw some flexibility in the circumstances, and the circumstances needn't have caused such deep guilt in me. This wasn't one of those life-threatening, black-and-white situations.

She gently placed her hand on my shoulder and said, "You're so dramatic, marriage boy." Amy lives with no regrets; reckless abandon is my wife. For the rest of the day she would whisper in my ear, "Ted, Jesus has set you free. Why do you live in this constant bondage to the past?" It's my guilt-prone nature. I can't change Amy. She can't change me. Every attempt to do so is futile. Each time we try, we waste our energy.

———— 💔 ————

In marriage, the first place many of us tend to look for fulfillment is to our mate. We think, *If I am to really have my needs met and be happy, I must have another person in my life.* However, those who expect a mate to fill the deepest needs ultimately will find that one human cannot charge another person's battery. A spouse can be frustrating and irritating and drain away as much, or more, emotional energy as they give. Our mate can be a tremendous source of help and encouragement, but even he can disappoint over the long haul. We can look to our spouse as the source of positive emotions, but at times she, too, can punch holes in our emotional lives.

Pledging not to expect your spouse to meet all of your

needs is a simple but powerful commitment that takes the pressure off your spouse. God never created Adam or Eve as a replacement for himself. Throughout the story of Creation, we read that God looked at the light, the water, the vegetation, and the animals, and they were all good. But when it came to the creation of man, which God called *very* good (emphasis added), God said it wasn't good for man to be alone. Man needed a suitable helper. Nothing in creation was an appropriate companion or counterpart to him. So God made the first woman.

But since the Fall and the eviction from the Garden, many men and women have tried to replace their relationship with God with their relationship with each other. We expect our spouse to become one of our main sources of life and joy. The result is codependence.

Codependence is created when we rely on people, places, or things to make or keep us happy. Codependents cope by blaming the other person for their unhappiness. We all have a tendency toward codependence. It sounds like this:

"If you would stop doing that, then I would stop."

"You started this argument."

"I said I do because I assumed you would too."

"We have money problems that are destroying our marriage."

"You are making me mad."

"If my husband would change a few of his annoying habits, we would have a much better marriage."

"If my wife would quit nagging, I'd do a lot better."

Whenever we begin to look to our spouse to meet all of our needs, we will be disappointed and feel let down. Eventually we'll feel unappreciated and even resentful. There are times in all of our relationships when we will feel like we're getting the short end of the stick.

Whenever your behavior is motivated by the action or reaction of your mate, you are setting yourself up for failure. You are to do the right thing no matter how your spouse responds or reacts. You are 100 percent responsible for you.

The absolute best thing you can do for your spouse's spiritual journey is to get off his or her case. Stop playing God in your spouse's life. Let your mate off the hook. Don't expect your mate to meet all of your needs. Make a commitment to do everything you can to drop your expectations.

Your mate was never created to form your deepest love, honor, or security. It's God's job to be our highest and best Friend and our loving King. All of the laws of Scripture can be boiled down to just two commandments (see Matthew 22:36-40): Love God and love others. It's a lot more hopeful and relaxing to know clearly what God's will is and that he will even give you the power to live it. He is love, and he gives love freely to those who crave to know and serve him. I try to start every day with the truth that God loves me more than anyone else does or can, and he desires to give me more and more of his power and love. I truly want to know him better today than I did yesterday. And I love hiding his powerful, living words within my heart in order to not only know him better but to do his will better.

Make God, not your mate, the center of your life. Imagine for a moment a blue plastic bucket. Now imagine that the bucket has a supply of clean, crystal-clear water from God. It never runs out. But unlike the bucket, your mate has limitations. Unlike the bucket, your mate will eventually run out. Your mate isn't going to have the energy to meet every one of your needs. Jesus told the lady who was coming with her bucket so that she could get water from the well that she was going to get thirsty again. But Jesus promised that if she drank from him, she would not thirst again (see John 4:4-14).

When you commit yourself to a vibrant relationship with God, you become like that blue bucket. You find yourself filled and refilled by God himself day after day. You find yourself renewed and ready to be poured out to your spouse, your family, and your community.

GARY... Before I get out of bed each morning, I like to quote Colossians 3:15 as a prayer: "Let the peace of Christ rule in your hearts." Why do I do that? So I'll be able to successfully practice Colossians 3:16, which advises, "Let the word of Christ dwell in you richly as you teach and admonish one another with all wisdom, and as you sing psalms, hymns and spiritual songs with gratitude in your hearts to God." When we practice simple spiritual disciplines like prayer, worship, and fellowship, we get filled up, and the peace of Christ rules in our hearts. When our focus is on God, then our spouses naturally get to enjoy the overflow.

When you are filled to the brim with God's love, the over-flow is a natural outpouring. You do not need to manufacture this love. And the fact is, you can't.

First Corinthians 13 speaks of this overflow. Just picture your spouse receiving this love from you:

"[Love] is not rude" (verse 5). Proverbs 18:13 shares a surefire recipe for rudeness: "Spouting off before listening to the facts is both shameful and foolish" (NLT). And Proverbs 17:28 says, "Even a fool is thought wise if he keeps silent, and discerning if he holds his tongue." Even a fool is thought to be a wise person when he guards his lips, when he watches his words, and when he uses more gracious words rather than rude, short, and to-the-point language.

"[Love] does not demand its own way" (verse 5, NLT). Love is understanding, not demanding. I have to learn to be understanding and quit pushing my own agenda. I have to stop thinking it's about me and my way, or getting to where I have to go and being there on my time.

"[Love] is not irritable" (verse 5, NLT). Gentleness goes a long way in marriage. Proverbs 15:4 says, "Gentle words are a tree of life; a deceitful tongue crushes the spirit" (NLT). Learn to deliver your words in a gentle tone. Remember, speed is the enemy of intimacy. A relaxed spirit will make you a gentler lover.

"[Love] keeps no record of wrongs" (verse 5). When you disagree with your spouse, do not bring up the entire his-tory of your marriage. Love lets go. It does not hold your mate in prison over past crimes, especially crimes for which the sentence has already been served. Refuse to remember it. Refuse to retaliate. Proverbs 19:11 (NLT) says, "Sensible people control their temper; they earn respect by overlooking wrongs."

Too often, couples believe that their happiness is based on each other. But our real happiness, our true joy, is based on our individual relationship with God. Couples often say they need help with their marriage, as if they don't have problems as individuals. In reality, when they get together their individual problems and sin manifest themselves. They blame their spouse or marriage for the issues, but the issues were in place before the marriage.

Some people believe their marriage is bad because they didn't marry their soul mate. That's simply not true. The concept of soul mates (sometimes referred to as twin souls) has its roots in the idea of reincarnation. Followers of this belief system hold that the soul of the one you are looking for has lived other lives with your past selves, and your souls have reconnected. Plato, an ancient Greek philosopher, referred to a soul mate as the other half. The concept of a soul mate has no biblical basis and sets up an excusable escape for couples.

I've had married people tell me, "Well, I think he is a great guy—he's just not the guy for me" and "I think she's wonderful and she'll make somebody very happy—she's just not making me happy." These are the wrong perspectives for sustaining a healthy marriage.

What are the right questions? Here is the foundation

for getting your marriage off on the right foot and staying there:

1. Am I demonstrating the loving image and character of Jesus Christ? If I'm not, I need to get his words into my heart so that I don't sin against God or my mate.
2. Have I taken responsibility for my own actions and reactions? If not, I need to get off my mate's case and get the help I need from God first and then from other wise counsel.
3. Do I understand that within me there is a self-destructive sin nature that only God can fix?
4. Do I understand that I make mistakes, I fail, and I grieve the heart of God?
5. Have I ever cried out to God as a beggar and admitted that I am helpless apart from him in becoming the mate I need to be?
6. Do I understand that because of Adam and Eve, I am now dealing with inherited sin?
7. Do I know that sin is basically doing my own thing and ignoring God?
8. When my spouse sees my deep love and transformation, will he or she want to join me on the spiritual journey?

The Bible says that "all have sinned and fall short of the glory of God" (Romans 3:23). We all deal with this issue of sin. The question is, how do we respond? Romans 10:9-10 instructs us to declare him as Lord (or as boss) of our lives and believe in our hearts that God has raised Jesus from the dead; then, the Bible says, we will be saved. It is a onetime decision (justification) followed by or made evident in life-style change (sanctification).

TED... When I ask couples to share their spiritual journeys, I am generally taken back to a time when they prayed a prayer, walked down an aisle, or stood up during a prayer at camp. I celebrate those decisions, but I also look for the fruit. I want to know about their spiritual journeys, not just their conversion times and dates. Too many couples treat their conversions as good enough and do not work to know God more. Because life change happens from the inside out, that is where marriage change begins as well. I am not concerned with a couple's parents' faith or the church they grew up in. I am interested in what they are doing today to know God.

The Bible says we are to submit to one another out of reverence for Christ (see Ephesians 5:21), because of what Christ has done. How then do we show gratefulness and thankfulness? Out of reverence for Christ, love your spouse—even when your spouse is unlovable. It's a mark of maturity. Remember that people, places, and things will never fill you up to overflowing. They are not the source of having your needs met. God, not your mate, is the only one who can meet all your needs.

It would be a great step for your spouse's spiritual journey to tell him or her that he or she is no longer in charge of your moods, emotions, words, or reactions. You will no longer blame your spouse for your shortcomings or hold him or her accountable for your spiritual journey. Step up to the plate and begin your journey of faith and feed it for yourself first. You are the CEO of your life, but you can ask your mate for assistance or help.

What if your spouse is not a believer? What about your spiritual journey then? First Peter 3:1-4 is an encouraging passage for those in that situation. It describes a believing wife married to an unbelieving husband and says that the husband will take notice of the change in her life. In other words, when you pursue the Lord with all your heart, soul, mind, and strength, you can't help but be transformed. When you are truly growing in the Lord, you will naturally become a more gentle, kind, and loving person. That means that you don't wait for your spouse to go to church, start reading the Bible, join a small group, or pray every day. Instead, you live your life as an example of those disciplines and Christ's grace. When you make every effort to seek your fulfillment from God, you'll find yourself not just lavished in God's love but also better able to lavish your spouse with love.

The real secret to creating more hunger in your spouse if he or she does not believe in God is by letting your mate see a model of someone becoming more like God without any signs of criticism from you about his or her behavior. Most people haven't seen a person who has hidden God's words within his or her heart and thus been led to godly transformation, or who has submitted to the Holy Spirit and thus has received amazing power to both love and bless others. When these two habits are formed in you, your unbelieving mate can discover the reality of God and his ways. When you're not being critical, your spouse gets to witness a real live model of God's transforming power in action.

Add your voice to the GPLL message . . .

Connect with us at www.greatparentslousylovers.com and watch the video podcast for chapter 10.

Post your thoughts, comments, and stories on our Web site. Here are some questions from chapter 10 to get you started on your journey to a couple-centered home:

- What have you been trying to change in your spouse?
- What change do you need to make in you?
- Why is it so easy to expect more out of our spouses and less out of ourselves?
- How can you communicate to your spouse this week that you are letting him or her off the hook?
- Take a few minutes to pray for your spouse right now. Ask God to bless him or her today.

FOLLOW-UP DATE:

Remember the character quality you committed to pray about in chapter 9? Don't forget to pray also for the trait your spouse is working on. Go out for coffee or dessert and surprise your husband or wife with a handwritten certificate that affirms signs of growth in their chosen quality. Then commit to verbalize those affirmations as you see the progress your spouse is making along his or her spiritual journey.

CHAPTER 11

YOUR CHILD'S
SPIRITUAL JOURNEY

You might be a Great Parent, Lousy Lover if it is more important
to you to have a child in the accelerated reading program or
on the honor roll, rather than to create a home where Mom and
Dad thoroughly enjoy each other.

THE GREAT PARENT, Lousy Lover generation has created what
Time magazine calls "helicopter parents." These are parents
who overprotect, smother, and invest too much in their kids.

Wait a minute! We can give our kids too much attention,
time, and resources? Short answer: yes.

"There is now a new revolution under way, one aimed
at rolling back the almost comical overprotectiveness and
overinvestment of moms and dads. The insurgency goes by
many names—slow parenting, simplicity parenting, free-
range parenting—but the message is the same: Less is more,
hovering is dangerous, failure is fruitful," says *Time* writer
Nancy Gibbs.[1]

In the last chapter we challenged you to get off your mate's case, and in some ways that is the same approach your kids need. I (Ted) must confess, I have a relaxed parenting style. It is a style that waits for those teachable moments and speaks truth when necessary. I don't try creating them; they just happen.

TED... Imagine watching a kid-friendly program on the Discovery Channel with your family. The show you are watching is celebrating God's creation of the earth. Okay, maybe they aren't giving God the credit, but the pictures of the earth in HD are amazing.

During one of the breaks, a commercial with a middle-aged man comes on, advertising a real solution for ED (a.k.a., erectile dysfunction). You scramble for the remote to find the mute button before your kids start listing the side effects and what to do if you have an erection lasting more than six hours.

The commercial repeats "ED" this and "ED" that for what seemed like a dozen times.

Then your kindergartener looks up with her baby-blue eyes and says, "Oh, Dad, two boys in my class have that problem."

What? you ask yourself while keeping a calm exterior.

"Sweetie, what do you mean?" you ask.

"Oh yeah, Dad, they go down to the nurse's station every day before lunch and get a couple of pills for that," she insists.

"Oh, honey, that's ADD not ED," you say with great relief.

Are you ready to answer questions your kids will ask after seeing those Cialis and Viagra commercials? God has placed me in the lives of Corynn and Carson to guard and shape their hearts. The world will throw many beliefs at them in their lifetimes, and I want them to discern the difference between God's truth and Satan's counterfeit. Remember what Proverbs 4:23 says about guarding your heart above all else? Everything about your life flows from your heart. Everything about your child's life flows from his or her heart.

I am thrilled that I could be with Corynn and answer boldly her questions about life and sex. Amy and I made the decision early on to tackle issues and questions head-on. Guarding their hearts means plain-and-simple honesty. That's why when our kids ask questions about their body or sex, we say it like it is.

I will never forget the night my three-year-old son popped up out of the bathtub looking at his penis and asked, "What is this?!" Depending on the parent, there is more than one answer to that question.

"That is your wa-wa."

"That is your tally wacker."

"That is your ying-a-ling."

"That is your front half."

Boldly I proclaimed, "That is your penis, Carson." I vaguely remember using a deep voice as well.

Wouldn't you know it, that became Carson's new favorite word. That next Sunday, between services at Woodland Hills, I went over to our children's department to check on my little guy. When I got to his class, the teacher was very standoffish.

She eventually got up the nerve to ask me, "Pastor, can I talk to you for a second?"

I said, "Sure, what's going on?"

She asked, "Is everything okay at home, everything good?"

I said, "Yeah, everything's great." What I didn't realize was that Carson had been using his new favorite word all morning.

Mom and Dad, whether it happens during a candid conversation over a Cialis commercial or a teachable moment at bath time, we get to impress messages on the hearts of our children throughout the day. What they learn from us, by word and deed, will sink deeply into their hearts. They will take it with them for the rest of their lives.

Deuteronomy 6:5-9 puts it this way, "Love the LORD your God with all your heart and with all your soul and with all your strength. These commandments that I give you today are to be upon your hearts. Impress them on your children. Talk about them when you sit at home and when you walk along the road, when you lie down and when you get up. Tie them as symbols on your hands and bind them on your foreheads. Write them on the doorframes of your houses and on your gates."

The message to be passed on to children is "Love the Lord" (verse 5). How that message is to be communicated is found in one word: "impress" (verse 7). We impress messages on our children's hearts every day, all day by what we say and do, from the time we get up until the time we go to bed (verse 7). As you go through your day, you are molding and shaping your children's hearts.

This Deuteronomy 6 teaching has led Woodland Hills Family Church to be an orange church. Orange is an inspiration of Reggie Joiner's reThink Group. He teaches the Orange principle with lemon drops and fireballs.

Imagine a large container filled with three thousand yellow lemon drops. Each lemon drop represents one hour of time a mom or dad spends with his or her child. The average parent interacts with his or her child three thousand hours a year. This does not include sleeping, school, or time with friends. These three thousand hours represent the average amount of time in a year parents engage or are in close proximity to their kids. There are 8,760 hours in a year, and Mom and Dad get the lion's share. The three thousand hours are represented by the color yellow.

Now, imagine forty red fireballs. The red fireballs represent the number of hours that church leaders, pastors, directors, volunteers, and teachers spend with your kids each year at church. That is how much time is given by the church to your children. Now this is the key to understanding.

When we first started as a church, like a lot of churches, we spun our wheels thinking of ways to maximize those forty red hours. We even strategized how to increase the number of hours from forty to fifty. Then it hit us, thanks to Reggie: We were blowing a humongous opportunity because nothing we were doing was focusing on the three thousand hours Mom and Dad spend with the children. Mom, Dad, you are going to impress a lot more in those three thousand hours than the church could ever imagine impressing in the forty.

The reason my kid calls somebody a moron because he or she cut us off in traffic is not because of the forty hours a Sunday school teacher spent with him in the classroom. It's because of the three thousand hours I spent with him.

The reason we call ourselves an Orange family ministry is because we want to maximize these forty hours to partner with Mom and Dad; our two combined influences are stronger than just one. It does not take a lot of red to turn yellow into orange. On Sundays, our church serves to drop a little red food coloring into every family that walks through the door. We are not a drop-off ministry. We are not a ministry that says to just bring us your kids and we are going to do the spiritual training.

Howard Hendricks at Dallas Seminary says this: "The church gets children one percent of their time in a given week. The school gets children 16 percent of the time. Mom and Dad and the home get children 83 percent of the time."

According to Deuteronomy 6, home is the primary discipleship-making tool for your children. Take responsibility for your children's spiritual growth by cultivating a strong and vibrant marriage. After all, your home starts with your marriage. You hear it all the time: "We are going to divorce and stay friends for the kids."

My answer to that little tidbit is this: "If you can stay friends for the kids, then you probably can stay married."

I have dedicated the rest of my ministry years and life to strengthening marriages because I believe great parenting is a natural overflow of great spouses and lovers.

Show your kids how to love like Christ does in Ephesians 5:25: "Husbands, love your wives, just as Christ loved the church and gave himself up for her." Your kids have a front-row seat to your marriage. You can share with them all of the Bible stories you want, and you can get them to memorize Scripture, but if your marriage does not reflect the love of Christ toward one another, you are missing the mark.

Jesus and the Couple-Centered Home

GARY... Our kids are always watching. Norma and I have always tried to maintain a couple-centered home, and at times our children have had to remind us of this.

When our children were little, we had only two vehicles—a car and a mini motor home. Our family car was used for all of our activities and appointments, and the RV was used for vacations and emergencies.

One afternoon I took Greg out to run some errands, leaving Norma at home with Michael and Kari. As they were preparing dinner, Norma realized they were missing a few essential ingredients. Her only choice of transportation was the RV. She never made it out of the driveway.

As Greg and I returned home, we noticed the commotion in the driveway. The scene dropped my heart into my stomach. Norma and the kids were standing next to the RV, which had a gaping hole in the top above the passenger's seat. I noticed all sorts of debris on the driveway and quickly realized that not all of it came from the RV. The shingles were my next clue. Norma had sheered off a large corner section of our roof. Gutter, shingles, underlayment, tar paper, and all. I was silent trying to get a grip on the situation. Greg and I remained in the car while I collected myself.

"What am I going to say? What am I going to do?" I asked myself, but Greg overheard.

"Why don't you do what you teach others to do, Daddy?" Greg asked. Now was not the time for him to get smart, and I could tell he was very sincere.

"What do I teach others to do, Greg?"

"You always tell us that people are more important than things," he responded. Ah, from the mouths of babes. It is amazing that, when your emotions take over, you can forget everything you believe so deeply.

As I got out of the car, Norma came around the side of the RV. I was calm, but Norma had no idea that I had just received a counseling appointment from our nine-year-old. As I went over to hug her, she melted in my arms.

"I had no idea how you would react to this," she said. "When the neighbors saw what happened they decided to stay outside to see how you would react."

I looked over to the neighbors and, with the same smile from my infomercial days, I waved as though everything was great, because it was.

I will never forget that day and the lesson I learned. My

marriage is on display, and not because I am a marriage and family author and speaker. My marriage is a testimony not only to my adult neighbors, but more importantly to my children. They have a front-row seat to the love Norma and I share.

Children raised in a couple-centered home more fully understand the gospel of Jesus Christ. God's love manifested in marriage speaks more to kids than any Sunday school lesson or sermon. This truth is the essence of Ephesians 5:25. Marriage is used as a word picture for God's love for the church. What is your marriage teaching your kids about Jesus?

We all want to raise loving children. We want to raise kids who love God and love others. I also want my kids to love the church. Jesus said, "A new command I give you: Love one another. As I have loved you, so you must love one another. By this all men will know that you are my disciples, if you love one another" (John 13:34-35).

I grew up in a church that taught that you will be known as a true Christian by the length of your hair, the Bible translation you carry, your style of clothes, tithing, and regular church attendance. Never once did I hear a message about how your marriage teaches your kids how to love. We are known by our love for each other. Is Jesus known in your home?

An enemy wants to destroy your home. He has his sights set on your marriage. His crosshairs are on your children, and he is using you to get to them. Do you believe that Satan has a battle plan for your home? Do not let this catch you off guard. Be prepared with your own plan to guard the hearts of your home.

On September 11, 2001, our country experienced an evil that caught us off guard. We were not prepared. We did not have the enemy sized up properly. Our guard was down. This comes right out of *The 9/11 Commission Report*:

> We learned about an enemy who is sophisticated, patient, disciplined, and lethal. The enemy rallies broad support in the Arab and Muslim world by demanding redress of political grievances, but its hostility toward us and our values is limitless. Its purpose is to rid the world of religious and political pluralism, the plebiscite, and equal rights for women. It makes no distinction between military and civilian targets. *Collateral damage* is not in its lexicon. . . .
>
> We learned that the institutions charged with protecting our borders, civil aviation, and national security did not understand how grave this threat could be, and did not adjust their policies, plans, and practices to deter or defeat it. . . . The test before us is to sustain that unity of purpose and meet the challenges now confronting us.
>
> We need to design a balanced strategy for the long haul, to attack terrorists and prevent their ranks from swelling while at the same time protecting our country against future attacks.[2]

This report reminds me of the warning for us to have a plan and to stand firm. It is found in Ephesians 6:10-13: "Finally, be strong in the Lord and in his mighty power. Put on the full armor of God so that you can take your stand against the devil's schemes. For our struggle is not against flesh and blood, but against the rulers, against the authorities, against the powers of this dark world and against the spiritual forces of evil in the heavenly realms. Therefore put on the full armor of God, so that when the day of evil comes, you may be able to stand your ground, and after you have done everything, to stand."

Satan is sophisticated, patient, disciplined, and lethal. He hates your family and the thought of your marriage modeling the gospel of Jesus. He will utilize everything in his arsenal to destroy your marriage. His strategy is to ruin not only your marriage, but also the future marriages of your children. He methodically attempts to tear apart your marriage and works for collateral damage.

We must understand how grave this threat really is. We have been given the armor of God to protect our marriages and families. It is not an accident that Ephesians 6:10-13 follows the Bible's central teaching on marriage and family in Ephesians 5:22–6:4. The test before us is to sustain the unity of purpose and meet the challenges now confronting us. We need to design a balanced strategy for the long haul, to put on the full armor of God and prevent Satan from future attacks. No weapon formed against us shall prosper.

Probably the best commentary I have ever read on

Ephesians 6 does not come out of a Bible commentary. It is the battle cry you hear when the U.S. Army graduates a new band of brothers. It is called the Infantryman's Creed:

I am the Infantry. I am my country's strength in war, her deterrent in peace. I am the heart of the fight, wherever, whenever. I carry America's faith and honor against her enemies. I am the Queen of Battle.

I am what my country expects me to be, the best trained soldier in the world. In the race for victory, I am swift, determined, and courageous, armed with a fierce will to win.

Never will I fail my country's trust. Always I fight on, through the foe, to the objective, to triumph over all. If necessary, I fight to my death.

By my steadfast courage, I have won 200 years of freedom.

I yield not—to weakness, to hunger, to cowardice, to fatigue, to superior odds, for I am mentally tough, physically strong, and morally straight.

I forsake not—my country, my mission, my comrades, my sacred duty.

I am relentless. I am always there, now and forever.

I AM THE INFANTRY!

FOLLOW ME!

Dad, the battle is raging for your marriage and home. I have a plan to guard my wife's and children's hearts. I will not back down, give up, or give in. Will you join me in leading and guarding our homes? Will you join me in fighting the enemy of our homes? Will you fight through fatigue and strife to guard and protect? Will you be relentless in this fight? Guys, we're called to lead in this battle (see Ephesians 5).

Your marriage is writing messages on your kids' hearts every day. Every week I pick up the pieces of broken marriages, couples who have had bad messages written on their hearts. Deuteronomy 6 says this love for God is to be impressed on our hearts. Mom and Dad, we have the equation of how we get to do that: from the time we get up in the morning to when we go to sleep at night and as we walk along the day. We get opportunities every single day to share with our young people what a love for God, a love for others, and a love and an honoring of his creation look like.

Let's show our kids what a marriage should look like.

Add your voice to the GPLL message . . .

Connect with us at www.greatparentslousylovers.com and watch the video podcast for chapter 11.

Post your thoughts, comments, and stories on our Web site. Here are some questions from chapter 11 to get you started on your journey to a couple-centered home:

- Is your marriage modeling the gospel?
- What parts of your marriage make Jesus shine through?

- What have you been expecting from your church and their forty hours with your child?
- How can you better use your three thousand hours with your son or daughter?
- Will you take personal responsibility for your child's spiritual journey? What are your first steps toward a battle plan for guarding your child's heart?
- What conversations do you need to initiate with your child this week?

SPIRITUAL-SAVINGS DATE:

Investing in your kids' spiritual lives is even more important than saving for their college fund. After they're in bed, turn off the TV and brainstorm specific things to pray for your children: salvation, passion for God, wisdom, faithfulness, purity, hope, joy, health, safety, discernment—the list could be extensive. Spend fifteen or twenty minutes thinking about this, then pray for your kids together. Praying together for the precious souls God has entrusted to you builds passion for each other. You're in this together—that's truly amazing grace!

CHAPTER 12

YOUR MARRIAGE JOURNEY

You might be a Great Parent, Lousy Lover if, before you leave the house, you ask your husband, "Do you need to go potty before we leave?"

TED... Disney World is the Cunninghams' happiest place on earth. Last summer we were visiting Disney when I experienced one of the best family meltdowns ever. I am proud to say, it was not our family. I have to admit, when I see another family melting down, a flood of emotions hits me. I feel relief that my children are acting like angels. I feel compassion knowing the pain that family is experiencing. And I usually end with fear that it could be my family any second.

We were racing through Epcot to secure our fast pass for the new Soarin' ride. About ten feet from the automatic doors, this lady plowed her stroller through our family group, cutting me off from Amy and the kids. As I attempted to reconnect with my family in the doorway, her husband cut me off again as he tried to catch up to his wife's very frantic, mean pace. The husband grabbed the frame of the stroller and jerked it out of his wife's hands. I jumped back prepared to go all Chuck Norris on them.

He looked at her and delivered the best line I have ever heard at a theme park: "You don't have a clue how to have a vacation."

Amy, twenty feet ahead of me by then, was standing at the entrance motioning for me to keep up. I motioned back a "Just give me a second" sign while a million clever sayings started popping into my brain, things I thought the Lord had given me to share with this couple. Does that happen to you? Their child was in the stroller, and the husband was going over a very detailed list on how to have a good time on vacation. He was right in her face, intensely explaining how to have fun and be spontaneous. I was in awe at the scene they were causing.

I said to myself, *I'm right here, and I haven't pastored anybody for like four days, so I'm going to just share a little tidbit. Maybe I can do some drive-by counseling.* Problem was that everything that was coming to my brain was so sarcastic. *Lord, do I give them the sarcasm?* I wondered.

As the wife stormed off, mad, with the stroller, it was just the husband and me. This was my time to be a friend to this guy. Amy went on to get our fast passes for the ride.

As the husband looked at me I simply said, "Welcome to the happiest place on earth."

He didn't crack a smile. I could tell he was embarrassed. But I continued by saying, "They don't show this in the brochures, do they? . . . This your last day?"

Breathless, he said, "We've been here a long time."

My second favorite line ever delivered at a theme park happened at Silver Dollar City. A dad got on his kids' case while racing through the park: "If you don't knock it off, I'm going to stuff you in that barrel."

My third favorite theme-park line was from a dad responding to an overly aggressive photographer at the park entrance. When the photographer asked if he could get a picture of the man and his family, the dad said in front of his children, "Are you kidding? I don't even want to be here with them right now. Why would I want my picture with them?"

Welcome to the happiest place on earth.

Amy and I suffer from a disease we call "crazy travel syndrome." We love the adventure of travel and planning vacations on Web sites like Expedia, Orbitz, Disney, and Kayak. Getting ready for the trip is an adventure. We enjoy packing. We sing on the way to the airport. Rental cars and new hotel rooms are the best.

It is the return that wears us out. That is when we find ourselves on a delayed flight at 1:00 a.m. with two sleeping kids on our laps, trying to figure out how we are going to get them to the car at the airport. That is when we ask ourselves, "What were we thinking!" The drive home from the airport is the longest hour of my life.

Crazy-travel syndrome is the state of being clueless on the

front end of a trip as to the pain and suffering at the end of a long vacation.

When we are booking a trip on Expedia's site, a little screen pops up while we are waiting for our flight options. It reads, "Because travel is an adventure." That pretty well sums up our marriage. We have our ups and downs and crazy turns along the way. We love anticipating each new day. Adventurers appreciate the little things as well as the big. Experiencing challenges together makes it more about the chase and less about the destination.

Just like our vacations, our marriages need two key elements to keep the adventure alive: anticipation and community. Anticipation gives us something to look forward to every day. Community gives us someone to experience life with.

Most of us had both anticipation and community at our weddings. We planned for months for one special day and the honeymoon to follow. Friends and family flew from all over the country to support us on that day. While every day cannot be a party, it can be an adventure.

There is a beautiful picture of a wedding in Song of Solomon 3. It is a word picture from Old Testament imagery: "Who is this coming up from the desert like a column of smoke?" (verse 6). This is an early reference to the children of Israel wandering in the wilderness. God's chosen people were led from place to place by his Spirit in the form of a pillar of cloud by day and a pillar of fire by night. Solomon and the Shulamite woman knew that God brought them to this point, just as God had brought the Israelites into the

Promised Land. He arranged their wedding. It was a holy moment, a divine appointment. God was the author of their relationship, and they were willing to put their marriage and wedding on display for all to see.

In every ceremony I perform, I like to move the bride and groom apart and point to the crowd and say, "You are here today not just for a party, not just to have fun and bring a gift, but to witness what is taking place here. You are here to witness a Christ-centered marriage, and you will hold this couple accountable to, first and foremost, their relationship to the Lord and their relationship to each other." Sad to say, many church weddings today serve more like a justice of the peace ceremony.

In this text, the couple is partaking in a sacrament, a holy moment. If you think of your wedding as only a legal transition from being unmarried to married, or as being only a party in which you shared love with your friends, think again. Your vows marked a big decision. That day of your adventure continued when you got home from the honeymoon. The wedding day is a Christ-centered deal.

Christian marriages have the potential of intimacy that the world cannot understand. When a couple chooses to put Christ at the center of their lives and take personal responsibility for their spiritual journeys, they create a bond that is not possible for the unbeliever. If you are married to a spouse who does not walk with Christ, there is hope. Scripture teaches that through you, your spouse can be influenced to change (see 1 Peter 3). Pray daily for that spiritual bond to be formed between you and your spouse. I learned about this bond while dating Amy at Liberty University.

Dewayne Carson was the campus pastor at the time, and he noticed that Amy and I were getting pretty serious. Amy was a resident assistant and had been a prayer leader under Pastor Carson's leadership. I was a spiritual-life director for my dorm and led weekly Bible studies. Dewayne gave me some personal advice that seemed to go against everything I had been taught.

He said, "Ted, I know you are dating Amy Freitag, and I want to warn you about something. Do not do devotions together or have extended times of prayer together."

"What?!" I asked.

"If you start going deep together spiritually, it will create some intense sexual pressure in your relationship," he shared.

Boy, was he right. You can see this play out in the first two chapters of Song of Solomon. Solomon and the Shulamite are dating and getting to know each other. She shares her insecurities of family history and struggles with her body. He uses this intensely personal information to build security and honor into the relationship. That foundation leads to an intense sexual desire, which is why Solomon warns in 2:7, "Do not arouse or awaken love until it so desires." As they begin growing together in their spiritual journeys, their physical desire increases.

The same happened with Amy and me. When we prayed

together while dating, it was usually over the phone. That way we could wait to arouse love until after our wedding.

You want to experience the best sex of your life? Tend to your own, personal spiritual journey. Take responsibility for your walk with God. Then give the overflow to your spouse. As my African American pastor friend Rick Rigsby likes to say, "Guys, when you lead your home spiritually, it will turn your wife into a freak." You know what he means.

Not only is your marriage to be Christ centered, but it is also to be surrounded by biblical community. In chapter 3:7-8 we see that Solomon did not show up to his wedding alone. He had community. "Look! It is Solomon's carriage, escorted by sixty warriors, the noblest of Israel, all of them wearing the sword, all experienced in battle, each with his sword at his side, prepared for the terrors of the night."

Solomon takes responsibility for his adventure and does some preparation. He wants his bride to know she will ultimately be protected under his care. "King Solomon made for himself the carriage; he made it of wood from Lebanon" (Song of Solomon 3:9). The cedars of Lebanon are strong, noble, secure, known throughout the land. "Its posts he made of silver, its base of gold" (verse 10), meaning he is going to be able to take care of her financially. "Its seat was upholstered with purple, its interior lovingly inlaid by the daughters of Jerusalem" (verse 10). He doesn't show up alone. He is showing that the banner over her is love (see Song of Solomon 2:4).

Song of Solomon 3:11 is an application of Genesis 2:24,

which you'll recall refers to leaving and cleaving. "Come out, you daughters of Zion, and look at King Solomon wearing the crown, the crown with which his mother crowned him on the day of his wedding, the day his heart rejoiced." A man must leave his father and mother in order to cling to his wife.

GARY... During the early years of our marriage, Norma and I lived on very little. I was finishing up graduate school in St. Paul, Minnesota, and working at a church as the youth minister. As you can imagine, I earned almost nothing in terms of a salary. To make ends meet, Norma collected green stamps. It was great; with each purchase at the grocery store we saved more and more stamps. We would look through the catalog and dream about the different household items we could trade in our stamps for. Of course, I wanted the color TV, and she wanted a rocking chair. Finally the day arrived when we had saved up enough stamps.

While in line to trade in our stamps, I thought I'd try one more time to convince her that we really needed the TV.

Thinking I was so clever, I asked Norma, "Without the TV, what are you going to do while rocking in your chair?"

"I don't want the rocker to watch TV," Norma explained.

"Then why do you want it?" I asked, confused. I should have stayed home because I'll never forget what ensued.

"I want it to rock our children," she said, so tender and nurturing.

"Children?"

Norma smiled. "Yes, children."

"Well, how many children do you want anyway?" This is the part that I wish I had one of those emergency pull cords that fighter pilots use to bail out in the event their plane is on fire. I was about to crash and burn!

In all the time we had dated, through the engagement, and now marriage, I had never asked her this.

"Five or six would be nice," Norma proudly announced.

"Five or six children?" I shouted, clearly shaken.

"No, dogs." Norma winked. "Yes, children. Why?" Again, this should have been another clue for me to bail out. Although I was in a tailspin, I still had time to save myself. But, no!

"I don't want to have that many."

That was all I needed to say. I only wanted two, and with my big goals for the future I couldn't see how we could have more than two. The other people in line certainly heard the explosion as I hit the ground at Mach two. We spent the next few minutes passionately debating the number of kids we were going to have. With each step toward the front of the line, we argued until Norma finally shut down. I was humiliated that we had melted down, and I'm sure the other people in line were embarrassed for us as well. When we reached the front of the line, what do you think we traded in our stamps for? The TV or the rocking chair? You guessed it—I'm not a complete doofus.

If you are like me, on some level, either consciously or

unconsciously, you walked into your marriage with each person having different plans for adventure. And although we are often unaware of these plans, they shape the way we live and relate to our spouses.

I once heard a pastor say there are basically three stages in marriage. Stage one is the Ideal. That's when everyone is excited, when love is grand, and "our marriage is going to be different!" But then along comes stage two. The Ideal becomes an Ordeal. This is when we realize that our Prince Charming has warts and that our Sleeping Beauty is not nearly so lovely once she wakes up. Then, far too often, along comes stage three. And that's when either one of the spouses begins wishing for a New Deal. Have you noticed that trend in our culture?

God actually had a plan for marriage from the time he instituted it. He has a huge dream for marriage. Jesus restates the dream in Matthew 19:5-6, "For this reason a man will leave his father and mother and be united to his wife, and the two will become one flesh. So they are no longer two, but one. Therefore what God has joined together, let man not separate."

So point one of God's plan is that you and your spouse, as husband and wife, would share this radical uniting together at the core of your beings, your hearts, your minds, your souls. God brought you together in a way that you will never be united with any other person on the planet. He has united two as one at the core of your being.

God's design is not that you would just stick it out and be miserable. God designed and desires you to have this fantastic and rare, one-flesh kind of love for a lifetime.

If you are married to an unbeliever or if the person you are married to professes Christ but does not live it out, don't lose heart. You may not be able to change that person, but God can. Etch the words of 1 Peter 3 on your mind: "Your godly lives will speak to them without any words. They will be won over by observing your pure and reverent lives" (1 Peter 3:1-2, NLT). The key to remember: You can't change your spouse.

Let your husband or wife see your love and care for him or her. Be vulnerable with your own struggles in life. Honesty and vulnerability are both within the spirit of 1 Peter 3. Above all else, hold out hope that God can still change you, your spouse, and your marriage. Watch what happens when your mate sees you growing and becoming more like Christ every day.

Add your voice to the GPLL message . . .

Connect with us at www.greatparentslousylovers.com and watch the video podcast for chapter 12.

Post your thoughts, comments, and stories on our Web site. Here are some questions from chapter 12 to get you started on your journey to a couple-centered home:

- How can you better make your marriage an adventure every day?
- Are you anticipating great things for your marriage? Is there hope for the future?
- Name two or three couples with whom you share biblical, supportive community. Do they have the freedom to speak into your life and marriage?
- Name two or three dreams you and your spouse have for the empty-nesting years. Where will you live? Where will you visit? How will you serve the church? What will your retirement years look like?

ADVENTURE DATE:

Get out of your comfort zone and enjoy the adventure of serving alongside each other. As a couple, volunteer in your community. Serve at a soup kitchen, visit residents at a nursing home, lead a small group at church, or go on a short-term mission trip together. Kingdom work is always a unique adventure.

CHAPTER 13

DREAM BIG

You might be a Great Parent, Lousy Lover if you have ever been tempted to look for greener grass on the other side. Keep in mind, where the grass is greener, there is a septic leak.

TED... My daughter loves sea turtles. I so badly want to take her to a real ocean with real turtles. I picture her swimming with the turtles and gently reaching for a flipper. The other night I had a strong desire to make that dream a reality, so I logged in to my American Airlines account to see how many miles it would take to get us to the north shore of Oahu, Hawaii. At the right time of year, I could get the whole family over there for one hundred thousand miles. I asked Corynn, "Do you think you can handle an eleven-hour flight from Dallas to Honolulu?"

"Eleven hours in the same plane? I probably should wait until I am at least twelve." That's six years away, but I am very thankful for her ability to think rationally about that length of travel.

Let's pause right there. Many parents, I being one of them, would end the conversation and go on to plan B. For us, that might mean a ninety-minute flight to Denver for skiing in the winter. Problem is, there are no sea turtles in Denver.

Our friend Kevin Leman lends the best insight on this type of dreaming when he talks about a child requesting a pony. Most parents would give the rationale and reasons why a pony makes no sense: "We live in the city"; "We would have to board the pony"; "Do you know how much it costs to feed a pony?" With questions like that we teach our kids to stop dreaming.

A better approach might be to say, "Wow, wouldn't it be fun to ride a pony every day after school? What would you name the pony? Wouldn't your friends enjoy riding the pony?"

I completely ignored Kevin's wisdom. I immediately went to the length of flight when I could have said, "Corynn, what would it be like to swim with real, live sea turtles? Could you imagine what would happen if we were swimming by a mommy and daddy sea turtle and their babies were following behind them? I hope we can go to the ocean someday together and enjoy the sea turtles."

We would never think of killing our children's dreams. We ask them questions like "What do you want to be when you grow up?" It does not matter what their answers are, we respond with, "Sure, you would make a great (fill in the blank)." Early in a life, dreaming is as easy as breathing. We don't have to think about it.

If we would not kill our kids' dreams, why do we kill our spouse's?

I can do the exact same thing with Amy that I did with Corynn and the sea turtles. I love HGTV's *Dream Home* that premieres every New Year's Day. My wife and I start anticipating the show in late November. Every January 1 around 9:00 p.m., after the kids are off to bed, we hit play on the DVR and unwind. We get so excited in the first few minutes of the show. About halfway through it, I look at Amy and go, "But you know they're going to have to pay a 32 percent gift tax on that."

She goes, "Oh, you're right."

Then I say, "On top of that, they will have to pay their income tax." By the end of the show, here's where I'm at: "I wouldn't even want it if they gave it to me."

That's when Amy looks at me and says, "Well, aren't you a bucket of sunshine to watch this show with."

As we grow older and experience unfilled dreams, we stop dreaming. We get to a place where we realize that not all dreams will be realized and not all of our goals will be met. Then we just stop dreaming altogether. We ask ourselves, *Why bother? Is it worth it?* The answer to that question is *yes*, it is still worth it.

Dreaming is to marriage what breathing is to life. Without dreams the marriage dies. Dreaming, in and of itself, is beneficial to your marriage. When Amy and I leave a movie that has been set in Ireland or Paris, we love sitting down with a cup of coffee afterward and talking about what it will be like to go there one day. Since there are not a lot of parents of preschoolers taking European vacations, we know that our dreams could take more than twenty years to be realized. That's okay. I may never go to Ireland. That's okay. Dreaming about Ireland still has value. Dreaming is fun, and we enjoy thinking about our distant future together.

We so easily talk ourselves out of dreaming because it feels irresponsible. After all, daydreaming is for children, right? We dreamed of being firefighters, doctors, and nurses. But as we grew up, our dreams began getting pushed back. People began telling us to stop daydreaming. How many teachers told you to stop daydreaming? I dreamed all the time in school.

Remember in chapter 5 where we looked at the grinder in Ecclesiastes? You and I are thrown into the grinder of life. The grinder represents all of the obstacles, hurdles, troubles, and difficulties we face in life. We begin to feel ground down. We brought all of those dreams into marriage as well. Dreaming pictures a special future for your marriage. You will need to lean on your hope for that special future when feeling the pressures of the grinder.

Don't let the grinder chew up your dreams or keep you from dreaming. Let's take a look at several benefits to dreaming in marriage.

First, dreaming raises your desire for each other.

It was very easy to keep desire alive when you were first married. Your dreams were filled with the physical pleasures of marriage.

Look at what it says in Song of Solomon 1:2-3: "Let him kiss me with the kisses of his mouth—for your love is more delightful than wine. Pleasing is the fragrance of your perfumes; your name is like perfume poured out. No wonder the maidens love you!" Some scholars believe the Shulamite woman is speaking here of his character. Other women want to be with Solomon, and she fully understands why because she desires him so much herself.

"Take me away with you—let us hurry!" (verse 4). With desire rising, she's saying, let's get going; let's run as fast as we can. Where? Not on a date to the movies, not to a nice restaurant, but look at where she wants him to take her away. To the bedroom. "Let the king bring me into his chambers" (verse 4). She is expressing desire physically and sexually for her soon-to-be husband.

Sex is one barometer of the marriage. It offers clues to how great the relationship is going and what you need to work on. The first, most important thing about dreaming is that it intensifies your desire for your spouse.

Second, dreaming fills your day with possibilities.

She says in verse 13, "My lover is to me a sachet of myrrh resting between my breasts." One commentary I read this week said she is actually picturing Solomon laying his head against her chest everywhere she goes. As she goes about her day, she can't get Solomon out of her thoughts.

I hate traveling alone. When I travel to speak at events without Amy, I constantly think about experiencing elements of that trip with her. If something funny is said, I think to myself, *Amy would get a kick out of that.* When I stay in a nice hotel room, I think, *Amy sure would appreciate this room and decor.* If I am driving down a new stretch of road, I think, *She sure would enjoy the view.* The essence of Song of Solomon 1:13 involves dreaming about the possibilities of experiencing life with your spouse.

Third, dreaming together keeps you from dreaming of others.
Look what she says in 2:3: "Like an apple tree among the trees of the forest is my lover among the young men." Among all the trees in the forest, she draws her shade from Solomon's tree.

I want to make sure that I am that fruit tree for Amy and that she draws her shade from me.

My six-year-old daughter is now drawing her shade from me. One day (thirty to forty years from now) I will walk down an aisle and will move her out from underneath my shade tree. I will tell her, "Corynn, I'm entrusting somebody else to be your shade tree."

Have you ever noticed how stoic the walk down the aisle is at a wedding? It's called the wedding march. The fact that it is called a march has always cracked me up. I think I understand a little better since I've had a daughter of my own. It is a death march, for Dad's role at least.

As a dad, I have been the guy who has dreamed with her for over twenty years. I've been the guy who ate the pretend cookies and went, "Mmmm, these are awesome!" I'm the guy who drank the water and acted like it was the best tea England had to offer. I'm the guy who brushed the doll's hair. I'm the guy who helped stuff forty-two Build-A-Bears and wished on the little red heart with her. Then I dreamed with her about what kind of sports she could do and what she could be and who she could become.

One day I'll replay those images as long-ago memories and tell myself that I was dreaming with her, and now I am about to remove my daughter from underneath my shade tree and give her to another shade tree. Now I get why that march is so slow and painful. Dad is in pain.

Verse 6 says, "His left arm is under my head, and his right arm embraces me." She dreams of his embrace. Her eyes are for no other.

I must ask you two questions: Do you provide good shade for your spouse? Are you living under the shade of your mate? Dreaming together raises our desire for each other and ultimately creates a broader canopy of shade. There is no need to go outside of the marriage relationship to find shade.

Fourth, dreaming creates excitement and anticipation.

Here's an idea for a very cheap date. Go to a bookstore, get a cup of coffee, and then find a magazine rack and pick out travel magazines. Backpacking, kayaking, *National*

Geographic, Northwest Travel, etc. We have a dream of raising our kids internationally and visiting places around the world. Not just to vacation, but to serve and to do ministry. So we pull all that out and just sit there and have a ball dreaming together. Dreaming is cheap. It may not cost you a dime, but the return on investment is huge. We have some travel dreams that may be ten years away and some that may never happen. But nevertheless, spending time with Amy, thinking about the possibilities creates a tight bond and brings us the excitement of anticipation.

Fifth, dreams may change, but don't ever stop dreaming.

As dreaming with your spouse builds excitement and antici-pation, guess what? Some dreams are going to be held off. A lot of times I will open an adventure magazine and see somebody backpacking in Switzerland, and I'm not doing that this month. But I'll look at her and go, "This is one for our fifties." I'm already dreaming of an empty nest. In the next fifteen years our desires and tastes will probably change, but that's okay as long as we continue dreaming.

Do you have an iPod with a docking station? You can bring sounds of the ocean into your bedroom. Try that. There are free apps for sleeping machines that have sounds from all over the world. A ninety-nine-cent download on iTunes and you are in Hawaii. There are a lot of creative things we can do to begin dreaming.

Scripture says many are the plans in a man's heart, but

God ultimately directs his steps (see Proverbs 16:9). Scripture is not down on you planning and dreaming with your spouse, but as far as what the future has in store for you, God will ultimately direct your steps. As we begin to dream about the future, we also look back and review our history. Our faith is boosted when we acknowledge that the storms, traumas, and difficulties were part of God's plan to get us to the present moment.

Dreams change much like the seasons. Solomon speaks of this in Song of Solomon 2:11-13: "See! The winter is past; the rains are over and gone. Flowers appear on the earth; the season of singing has come, the cooing of doves is heard in our land. The fig tree forms its early fruit; the blossoming vines spread their fragrance. Arise, come, my darling; my beautiful one, come with me."

The winter is over; spring is here. You are entering a new season of your life. No matter what season you're in, never stop dreaming. When you believe a dream is dead, move on to the next one. Keep dreaming and asking each other, "Wouldn't it be cool if . . . ?"

Sixth, dreaming arouses curiosity toward your spouse.

When Amy and I listen to each other's dreams, we discover aspects of each other we never knew. Discussing our dreams raises our curiosity about each other. Amy has a huge plan to go to Europe. She can picture us sipping tea in England and walking through the fields of Ireland. I still have a dream for an RV. I want to load up the family some summer and head west.

When we are in the process of dreaming together, I learn about my spouse. Solomon puts it this way in chapter 2: "My dove in the clefts of the rock, in the hiding places on the mountainside, show me your face, let me hear your voice; for your voice is sweet, and your face is lovely" (verse 14).

The best way to draw your dove (a.k.a., spouse) out of the clefts of the rock is to ask great questions. You discover your spouse at deeper levels when you break outside of the familiar routine. Dreaming about the future is a great teacher to your marriage.

Seventh, dreams can be destroyed overnight. (Protect them!)

Up to this point in the Song of Solomon text, the couple is high on love. They are dreaming about each other; they want to be together sexually; they want to be together physically; they can't wait to explore each other's bodies. Again, dreaming creates intense desire.

Song of Solomon 2:15 states, "Catch for us the foxes, the little foxes that ruin the vineyards, our vineyards that are in bloom." In those days foxes were the most destructive animals to the vineyards. They could destroy an entire vineyard by eating the buds before they bloomed. If they ate enough buds, they could wipe out an entire crop.

Your vineyard is your marriage, and the foxes represent anything that can undermine growth and fruitfulness. The "foxes" that destroy our dreams are duty and responsibility. We get in that grinder and realize that dreaming just doesn't seem practical. Routine is another fox we must guard against. We grow comfortable with each other, and we allow things to drift.

We have to identify the foxes and be on guard against them. If your parents told you to stop dreaming, dream anyway. If your dreams can't be realized in your hometown, consider a move. Even if it's not possible to pick up and go right now, keep dreaming. Don't let culture and society tell you that dreaming equals irresponsibility. Faithfully following the Holy Spirit's call on your heart actually shows great maturity.

We want to help you to begin dreaming again. We have included in this chapter a series of questions, some fun, some dead serious, that will help you draw out your "dove." You can text, Facebook, tweet, or take them to dinner with you. Whatever you do, start dreaming. Start asking each other great questions.

Add your voice to the GPLL message . . .

Connect with us at www.greatparentslousylovers.com and watch the video podcast for chapter 13.

Post your thoughts, comments, and stories on our Web site. Here are some questions from chapter 13 to get you started on your journey to a couple-centered home:

- Can you name two or three dreams that have been lost in your marriage?

- Do you ever catch yourself dreaming about a life with someone else?
- What relationships do you need to end today to begin building back dreams with your spouse?
- What are your new dreams?
- Listed below are fifty-one questions to get you dreaming together as a couple. Start with just a few and get that dream muscle moving again.

DREAMING QUESTIONS

Work & Play

1. At this point in your life, which would you choose to make your life better: *better physical health, better relationships, more money, different job?*

2. If you could rewind to any point in your life, what would you want to relive? Would you enjoy it the same or change it?

3. What would you do if you didn't have to work?

4. What award would you like to win and for what achievement?

5. When do you feel most alive?

6. If you could try out any occupation for a year, what would it be?

7. How would you spend a perfect day alone?

8. You must choose four vacations—all expenses paid, of course—to take with your spouse. Each has a theme: Most Romantic, Most Fun, Most Adventurous, Most Relaxing. Where would you go for each?

9. What would you do with ten million dollars?

10. If you could take lessons to become an expert at anything, what would it be?

11. Hollywood called. They want to make a movie about you. What would it be about and who would play you?

12. If you could be a professional athlete, regardless of age or physical ability, what sport do you think you would enjoy the most?

13. Describe your dream house.

Fun & Leisure

1. If you could have dinner with three famous people, living or dead, who would they be?

2. Name something you love that no one else seems to like. Or, vice versa, name something everyone seems to love except for you.

3. Of the following adventures, which would you choose first and why? a) snow skiing; b) cheese-and-wine night; c) spelunking; d) movie night; e) a pro sports event; or f) camping?

4. If you could have a magic power, what would it be?

5. Sing the chorus or one line of your spouse's favorite love song.

6. What's the greatest invention of your lifetime?

7. What TV sitcom family would you be a member of?

8. What is one item you know you should get rid of but never will?

9. What were your favorite toys as a child?

10. Where do you most enjoy sitting outside your house?

11. Name three countries you'd like to visit.

12. What celebrity annoys you most?

13. Describe your dream car.

Love & Romance

1. What causes the most stress or conflict in your marriage: financial decisions, sexual expectations, parenting styles, value differences?

2. What positive thing do you not say enough to your spouse?

3. What would you do with your spouse for the next ten years if you knew they were your last?

4. Name one way your spouse makes you feel secure.

5. Name one thing you miss about your dating relationship.

6. How would you describe your spouse to a stranger?

7. What is the sweetest thing your spouse has ever said to you?

8. If you had an entire day to spend alone with your spouse, how would you spend it?

9. Who proposed, and how was it done?

10. How did you and your spouse meet?

11. What's the most romantic scene from a movie you can think of?

12. What is your perfect Valentine's Day date?

13. What's the most romantic season of the year?

All about You

1. How would you like people to describe you at your funeral?

2. Tell about an experience that was difficult but necessary in making you the person you are today.

3. What is your religious background? In what way has it affected you most?

4. If you wrote a book about your life, what would it be called?

5. What makes you most humble?

6. Name a song that you could really relate to at some point in your life.

7. What scares you the most?

8. What is the most honest thing you have ever done?

9. What's the best advice someone ever gave you?

10. What makes you most uncomfortable: being around new people, formal occasions, speaking to a large group, thong underwear?

11. On a scale of 1 to 10, how "cool" are you?

12. Tell about a favorite childhood memory you made with your family.

DREAM DATE:

Big dreams for down the road are vital, but so are smaller dreams you can pursue in the here and now. These more immediate dreams provide stepping-stones to get you from one stressful day to the next; they keep you hopeful while everything else is keeping you hopping. Plan a date for next week and jot it on the calendar. Then each day between now and your date, do one thoughtful act of service for your mate. Get up at night with the baby; rub your spouse's feet; do one chore he or she usually handles.

CHAPTER 14

PLAY HARD

You might be a Great Parent, Lousy Lover if you have told your family that they are going on a family vacation and you demanded that they have a good time.

GARY... When my children were young, one of the ways we connected with each other was by taking camping trips as a family.

We lived in Chicago at that time, and we borrowed a pop-up camper and drove to Pensacola, Florida. Our first night out was in Kentucky, where we had a little fire and s'mores under the pine trees. We had two kids at the time, and after we put them to bed, we kept talking.

After a while I said, "This is really nice. I like this." Then we went to bed.

All of a sudden the wind started blowing. Then it started raining, and then it was pouring. Then it was seeping through the cracks in the seams and dripping on us. Neither Norma nor I were moving because it was thundering and lightning and blowing. It was a huge storm. I couldn't remember whether we were in the middle of a gully, and I didn't know if we were going to get washed away. We held hands, and about halfway through the storm, she said, "Do you think we are going to blow over?"

"Nah," I answered. I thought we were going to blow up, not over. I thought we were going to die. We made it, though, and we both thought to ourselves that camping can't be the secret to close-knit families.

So then we made it to Florida and the kids went wild. There was sand in the beds and in the food. I tried to surf and fell off, and the surfboard went under the water, then came back and split me totally open. A fellow surfer looked at me in shock and said, "I really don't know you that well, but I think you ought to have that checked out." I was numb, so I really couldn't tell.

We didn't have any money, so when I got back to the camper I cut a bandage and made a little butterfly thing and put stuff on it. Norma thought everything was funny that night. I couldn't laugh; I was just miserable. I thought, *This is horrible. This is not making us closer. We can't stand each other right now, so let's go home. We can't stand the kids; let's get out of here.* By the time we got to about two hours out of Chicago, the kids were just irritating both of us. We agreed we would never camp again.

We stopped at one of those Stuckey's restaurants and

bought gifts for the kids. Greg got one of those spring-loaded guns—the kind with soft tips on the "bullets." Of course, he immediately took off the soft tip and shot it. It ricocheted and hit Norma in the ear. I had to pull over and grab her because she was going back to strangle him. When we got home, we breathed a collective sigh: "Ahh, finally. Never again."

Then something very interesting happened. About three weeks later, when we had all forgiven each other and got the anger out of us, we started laughing about those experiences. We started really laughing, and we laughed for quite a while. I couldn't even figure out what was going on because I didn't really understand it. But we didn't really have to. . . .

Camping is scheduled disasters. We now know from research that going through a disaster together bonds people.

I knew that every time we went camping, something was going to go wrong. I didn't know what it would be. Sometimes it was really bad; sometimes it was just a little bit bad. I could go on for hours about the disasters we experienced camping, but those shared disasters are the value of the experience.

---------- 💜 ----------

Life is a lot like camping; something is always about to go wrong. Solomon refers to this as the grinder in Ecclesiastes 1:4-7: "Generations come and generations go, but the earth remains forever. The sun rises and the sun sets, and hurries back to where it rises. The wind blows to the south and turns to the north. . . . All streams flow into the sea, yet the sea is never full."

The earth is a grinder that we are born into. Life is hard. Life is full of challenges, full of difficult times, full of pain. You are in the grind until your body starts breaking down and you die (see Ecclesiastes 12).

In Genesis 1, God creates the heavens and the earth and declares at the end of each day that "it is good." In chapter 2, he creates man and woman, male and female, puts them in this playground called the Garden, and says, "Enjoy each other and enjoy all of this, but here's the one thing I don't want you to do: don't eat of that tree."

Then Satan comes in and tells them they can eat of it and that what God told them wasn't true. Actually he says their eyes will be opened and they will become like God. So Eve takes it and then asks Adam to take a taste. Enter God.

God knows about the grind.

Guys, God knows the struggle of providing for your family. He pronounced it in the Garden. He knows that earning a living is a challenge. He knows about this grind that Solomon talks about in Ecclesiastes 12. He knows about the mantle of duty and responsibility resting on your shoulders.

We read about the struggle in Genesis 3:17-19: "To Adam [God] said, 'Because you listened to your wife and ate from the tree about which I commanded you, "You must not eat of it," Cursed is the ground because of you; through painful toil you will eat of it all the days of your life. It will produce thorns and thistles for you, and you will eat the plants of the field. By the sweat of your brow you will eat your food until you return to the ground, since from it you were taken; for dust you are and to dust you will return.'" Work is going to be hard. Providing is going to be very, very difficult for you, as it was for Adam.

Flip over with us to Ecclesiastes, where Solomon says this in 3:9 (keep in mind that God knows about the grind): "What does the worker gain from his toil?" Let us give you some images for toil. The New American Standard Bible actually uses the term *labor* in Ecclesiastes 3:13. It's the same when we're talking about giving birth, which is what was put on women. Women will have labor during childbearing. Men, when you work it will be labor. The word means trouble, anguish, misery, and sorrow—hard work. What does the worker gain from all of this trouble, anguish, misery, and sorrow?

Again, God did not give you your spouse to be a part of this grinder. He gave you your spouse to go through the grinder with you. If you see your spouse as the grinder, you start to view him or her as the enemy.

You're in the grind all the way to the end.

GARY... As you grow older, the grinder seems to intensify. For me, staying alive is a part-time job. When I travel, I carry an entire bag of life-saving equipment to keep me alive at night. You know you're getting old when you check your life-support system at the airport.

Some of you have surpassed the seventy, or even eighty, years that Moses said we have (see Psalm 90:10). Blessings to you. Some of you are a few years away from this. Moses also says in verse 10, "Yet their span is but trouble and sorrow, for they quickly pass, and we fly away." Life is hard, you die, and you mourn. So the grind lasts for your entire life. More money can't purchase an escape from the grind. More education can't outsmart it. It is in your life, and marriage, up until the very end. That is why you need to learn to play.

Play in the midst of the grind.

Remember Ecclesiastes 9:9? It says to "enjoy life with your wife." If you are among the living, you have hope. You can have a great marriage. You can enjoy life with your wife, "eat your food with gladness, and drink your wine with a joyful heart" (Ecclesiastes 9:7).

God is so serious about the idea of enjoying life with your wife that he turned it into law. Deuteronomy 24:5 reads, "If a man has recently married, he must not be sent to war or have any other duty laid on him. For one year he is to be free to stay at home and bring happiness to the wife he has married."

Think about this, ladies, for just a second. God is saying that keeping you happy is a full-time job. Are you picking up on that? Guys, you can relate to this because you have a full-time job, your marriage is a full-time job, and you have a couple of full-time jobs we call children.

There was a study several years ago in which they asked two thousand wives what their husbands do that gets them in the mood. Do you know what the number-one answer was? Domestic support gets women in the mood. Ted regularly tells me the sound of him vacuuming is foreplay in their home. Now watch how domestic support can work in your home.

God put within us a powerful love hormone called oxytocin that begins to wash over our brain when we play together with those we love. One couple figured out that one of their favorite playtimes was the one or two hours every Saturday they cleaned house together. They would turn music on as loud as they could, and they would sing as they cleaned. They didn't know what was happening, but they were actually coating their brains with oxytocin. Laughing together releases the love chemical as well.

If you will play together for just twenty minutes a day, you will decrease your chances of divorce.

Oxytocin is a tremendous motivator for intimacy. So when that love hormone is at work, it almost forces you to want to be with that person you're playing with. You want to be bonded, you want to cuddle, and you want that chemical that God gave you to flow. It flows while we play, but guess what else happens? It melts away anger naturally. Oxytocin is so pleasurable that whatever you may have been upset or angry about seems to fade away. When you play and have fun and laugh together, your brain is relieved of tension and stress.

I love watching children play. When Norma and I meet Ted and Amy for lunch, their son, Carson, usually joins us. Carson loves Legos. He brings a bag of them everywhere he goes. He can spend all day building things with them. Do you know why? Because he ain't got a job. He can spend all day playing with Legos because he ain't got no duty or responsibility.

The bottom line is this: You know how to play. You need breaks, however small they may be, from duty and responsibility to let your heart be carefree. You can be creative. When you were a kid, you played with Legos, Lincoln Logs, and Pick-up Sticks. I watch as Carson plays with those Legos and think about him growing up. He will one day be introduced to duty and responsibility. As he grows, he will drift away from play and move toward responsibility.

Have duty and responsibility trumped fun in your marriage? Have you stopped living and enjoying life with your spouse? The key is not to replace play and fun with duty and responsibility. We must balance them all. Keep a regular date night reserved for playtime. Revisit some of the places you frequented on your first dates. If they are too far away, reminisce about your favorite restaurants, past vacations, honeymoon spot, and so on. After forty years of marriage, I am still finding out new nuggets about Norma as we play together. I love playing with her more than anything.

Add your voice to the GPLL message . . .

Connect with us at www.greatparentslousylovers.com and watch the video podcast for chapter 14.

Post your thoughts, comments, and stories on our Web site. Here are some questions from chapter 14 to get you started on your journey to a couple-centered home:

- How are you feeling the grind this week?
- What are some escape mechanisms we use in the midst of the grind?
- Why does play feel irresponsible to adults?
- If you can't enjoy life, you can't enjoy your spouse. What can you do today to better appreciate and enjoy life?

PLAY DATE:

Go for a walk, enjoy a cozy movie night, or go out to dinner with friends. Discuss absolutely nothing heavy, and enjoy being fun and flirtatious together.

CHAPTER 15
LAUGH MORE

You might be a Great Parent, Lousy Lover if the majority of laughter in your home comes from a pop star with a split personality or a sponge that lives under the sea.

TED... Preacher Henry Ward Beecher says, "A marriage without a sense of humor is like a wagon without springs—jolted by every pebble in the road. Humor makes all things tolerable."

"Laugh out loud," says Chuck Swindoll. "It helps flush out the nervous system." On another occasion Chuck said, "Laughter is the most beautiful and beneficial therapy God ever granted humanity."

Psychoanalyst Martin Grotjahn, author of *Beyond Laughter*, notes that "to have a sense of humor is to have an understanding of human suffering."

Bob Hope says laughter is an "instant vacation."

Jay Leno says, "You can't stay mad at somebody who makes you laugh."

Bill Cosby says, "If you can find humor in anything, you can survive it."

Essayist and biographer Agnes Repplier, who was known for her common sense and good judgment, said, "We cannot really love anybody with whom we never laugh." I agree.

My mission in life is to make Amy Cunningham laugh. One way in which I accomplish this is by modeling my wardrobe choice for her each morning. After dressing, I step out of the closet and put my hands on the corner of the vanity. Then I drop my head like one of those New York runway models and lean my back end toward Amy and say, "You want to tap it?" Trust me, it is not a sexual move. She breaks into laughter every time.

Try it sometime. You can dance. You can model. You can sing. Anything that takes you out of your comfort zone will usually do the trick.

Not taking yourself so seriously is the first step toward bringing laughter into your marriage. Being a responsible adult does not mean that you must remain serious at all times. Rather than masking your weaknesses or imperfections, try being honest about them. After all, your spouse knows all of your weaknesses. Self-deprecating humor goes a long way in building intimacy in your marriage.

My mentor in this area has been Dr. Chuck Swindoll, pastor of Stonebriar Community Church in Frisco, Texas. I attended Dallas Seminary during the years he was president of the school. I have always appreciated Dr. Swindoll's sense of humor and how he used it regularly in his messages. He often shared about fights he had with his wife, but he always took the blame. He used self-deprecating humor to take responsibility for their marital strife.

What I didn't know was that Dr. Swindoll almost did not go into ministry because of his love for laughter. In my favorite book of Dr. Swindoll's, *Laugh Again*, he challenges us to lighten up and open our hearts to laughter:

> My question is this: When did a healthy, well-exercised sense of humor get sacrificed on the altar of adulthood? Who says becoming a responsible adult means a long face and an all-serious attitude toward life?
>
> My vocation is among the most serious of all professions. As a minister of the gospel and as the senior pastor of a church, the concerns I deal with are eternal in dimension. A week doesn't pass without my hearing of or dealing with life in the raw. Marriages are breaking, homes are splitting, people are hurting, jobs are dissolving, addictions of every description are rampant. Needs are enormous, endless, and heartrending.
>
> The most natural thing for me to do would be to allow all of that to rob me of my joy and to change me from a person who has always found humor in

life—as well as laughed loudly and often—into a stoic, frowning clergyman. No thanks.

Matter of fact, that was my number-one fear many years ago. Thinking that I must look somber and be ultraserious twenty-four hours a day resulted in my resisting a call into ministry for several years. I distinctly remember wrestling with the Lord over all this before He pinned me to the mat and whispered a promise in my ear that forced me to surrender: "You can faithfully serve Me, but you can still be yourself. Being My servant doesn't require you to stop laughing."

That was all I needed to hear. God has given me a sense of humor and I can bless my spouse and children by making them laugh.[1]

God wants you to laugh.

In the last chapter we saw how we need to learn to play in the midst of the grind. We also need to learn to laugh in the midst of the grind. The grind may be one reason why the average child laughs some four hundred times per day compared to the average adult laughing only fifteen times a day. If we let it, the grind can rob us of our sense of humor.

Solomon shares with us that laughter is an important season of life and a break from the grind. Laughter is given to us as a time of refreshment, just like the seasons: "There is a time for everything, and a season for every activity under heaven" (Ecclesiastes 3:1). God has appointed the seasons of our lives. They are part of his creation.

We have seasons from God, the One who created the heavens and the earth. He put the earth in rotation around the sun. He set the earth on an axis of 23.5 degrees. That's what gives us our seasons. The Creator did this for us, and he says in verses 2 through 3 that there is an appointed time to be born. There is an appointed time to die. There is an appointed time to plant and an appointed time to uproot. There is an appointed time to kill, an appointed time to heal, an appointed time to tear down, and a time to build.

He has even given us an appointed time to laugh (see verse 4). The almighty Creator of heaven and earth gave us laughter as a season. In extreme climates, there are really only two seasons, a rainy season and a dry season. If you have young children at home, you get the idea of a dry season for your marriage. You are just going through the motions. I know, I have a four-year-old and a six-year-old. I'm in a season of preschoolers.

Some of you are in the empty-nest season. My friend Mark Connelly, pastor of Mission Community Church in Gilbert, Arizona, is a brand-new empty nester. We are partnering in this new marriage ministry to ignite married couples through adventure. A few months back Mark encouraged the married couples in his congregation to enjoy sex with each other more often and with more passion. (We'll get to that in chapter 17.) Mark and I both came up with the idea to create a menu that had fifty questions about sex. The idea was for couples to take this menu home after the message and have a deep conversation. Probably a conversation many have never had.

Mark came up with the idea to give each couple a two-hour burning candle. They were to go home, light the candle, and talk for two hours about sex. When I heard this, I died laughing.

I scolded Mark in front of his entire church the next time I visited out there to speak: "It is obvious your pastor is an empty nester. What planet is he living on? Get real, Mark! Who has time to talk about sex for a couple of hours?"

The congregation validated my observation. I didn't stop there. I continued by saying, "Let me help all of my friends in the young-children season of life. If you light that candle Mark gave you and place it under a ceiling fan on high power, the conversation will go a whole lot faster."

Seasons are good because they give us something to look forward to. We learned in chapter 7 that God gave us a little break each week to allow us to refresh and renew. He has planned your life with a variety of seasons.

What season is your marriage in right now? Is it in one of those dry seasons where everything is a fight? Can I be blunt? Some of you are currently in a "too serious" season. Laughing to you seems childish and immature. Lighten up. Your spouse will thank you, and you will live longer.

I think somewhere along the line Christianity has taught that marriage and adulthood are about long faces and being serious all the time.

How else is laughter good for you? Let's look at Proverbs

17:22, which states that "a cheerful heart is good medicine, but a crushed spirit dries up the bones." How many of you could use a little dose of a cheerful heart? Laughter not only benefits your marriage, but it also benefits your health.

The healing power of laughter was not taken seriously by a scientific world until the late Norman Cousins, former editor of *Saturday Review* and subsequently professor at UCLA's School of Medicine, wrote about his life-changing experience with humor. As he reported in his book *Anatomy of an Illness*, laughter helped turn the tide of a serious collagen disease. "I made the joyous discovery," Cousins reported, "that ten minutes of genuine belly laughter had an anesthetic effect and would give me at least two hours of pain-free sleep." He surrounded himself with Marx Brothers films and *Candid Camera* videos. He also checked out of the hospital and moved into a hotel where, as he says, he could "laugh twice as hard at half the price."

Cousins called laughter "inner jogging" because every system in our body gets a workout when we have a hearty laugh. Laboratory studies support Cousins's hunches. Our cardiovascular and respiratory systems, for example, benefit more from twenty seconds of robust laughter than from three minutes of exercise on a rowing machine. Through laughter, muscles release tension, and neurochemicals are released into the bloodstream, creating the same feelings the long-distance joggers experience as "runner's high."

Your home needs laughter to reduce stress, improve health, and create a bond with your spouse and children. For years

Gary taught the principle that feelings follow actions. Do the right thing, and the feelings will catch up.

So we want you to start laughing even if you cannot find anything to laugh about. Do it right now. Just tighten up your stomach and start laughing. You can actually fake laughing even if you don't feel like laughing. Have you ever noticed that spontaneous laughter is contagious for your family? Somebody starts laughing and then you start laughing. You walk into a room where people are laughing, and it immediately brings a smile to your face. That is the power of laughter.

Add your voice to the GPLL message . . .

Connect with us at www.greatparentslousylovers.com and watch the video podcast for chapter 15.

Post your thoughts, comments, and stories on our Web site. Here are some questions from chapter 15 to get you started on your journey to a couple-centered home:

- Is there a vacuum of laughter in your home?
- In what areas of life do you need to lighten up?
- Do you take yourself too seriously? In what ways?
- Think of a favorite joke from the past. We would love for you to share it on our Web site. Help us ignite other couples with laughter.

So let's take some of this medicine together. Listed below are some one-liners to get you started on your dates . . .

If the new American father feels bewildered and even defeated, let him take comfort from the fact that whatever he does in any fathering situation has a fifty percent chance of being right. || BILL COSBY

Human beings are the only creatures on earth that allow their children to come back home. || BILL COSBY

Women don't want to hear what you think. Women want to hear what they think—in a deeper voice. || BILL COSBY

If airline seat cushions are such great flotation devices, why don't you ever see anyone take one to the beach? || JERRY SEINFELD

Politics: "Poli" a Latin word meaning "many" and "tics" meaning "bloodsucking creatures." || ROBIN WILLIAMS

I don't like country music, but I don't mean to denigrate those who do. And for the people who like country music, denigrate means "put down." || BOB NEWHART

The laziest man I ever met put popcorn in his pancakes so they would turn over by themselves. || W. C. FIELDS

Changing a diaper is a lot like getting a present from your grandmother—you're not sure what you've got but you're pretty sure you're not going to like it. || JEFF FOXWORTHY

My wife is so analytical with raising kids, and I am not. My feeling is if they turn out good, then that means I was a good daddy and put a lot of effort into it. If they turn out bad, it means they took after her side of the family. || JEFF FOXWORTHY

Life is a little easier for attractive people. Think about it, if a stranger smiles at you and they're attractive, you think, "Oh, they're nice." But if the stranger's ugly, you're like, "What do they want? Get away from me weirdo." || JIM GAFFIGAN

I haven't spoken to my wife in years. I didn't want to interrupt her.
|| RODNEY DANGERFIELD

My psychiatrist told me I was crazy and I said I want a second opinion. He said okay, you're ugly too. || RODNEY DANGERFIELD

I realized recently that what I need to find is a woman who loves me for my money but doesn't understand math.
|| MIKE BIRBIGLIA

I was at the breakfast table this morning and read that more and more adults are living with their parents. I was like, "Mom! Did you read this?" || BRIAN REGAN

I took a speed reading course and not to brag but my speed shot up to forty-three pages a minute. But my comprehension plummeted.
|| BRIAN REGAN

CHILDLIKE DATE:

Sit down together and have fun reviewing happy memories in your relationship or cute things your kids have said or done. While your kids aren't the focus of these dates, they do provide endless reasons to laugh about their antics, expressions, and words. Browse photo albums or scrapbooks to refresh your memory.

CHAPTER 16

TOUCH OFTEN

You might be a Great Parent, Lousy Lover if you have ever had a kiss interrupted by a kid screaming, "Mommy, can you help me wipe?"

TED... Emma asked her mom and dad, "Why don't you guys kiss more?"

"We do kiss when you're not around," Stephanie responded.

"Well, if you are in love, you should kiss a lot more," Emma insisted.

Andy chimed in with, "I, too, think we should kiss more, Emma."

Stephanie eventually gave in and leaned in for a kiss. As their lips touched, six-year-old Emma led her brothers and sister in a cheer. "Go Dad, go Dad, kissing scene, oh yeah!"

Meaningful touch has never been easy for me. My wife

does not have a huge need for it either. Neither one of us has it as a love language. Touching I can do. Being touched is tough.

My first and last massage was in February 2009 in northern California. What was I thinking allowing California to be the first state to give me a massage? Don't hate me, California, but it was one of the most horrible predicaments of my life.

Amy and I were doing a marriage retreat for Cornerstone Fellowship in Livermore. Caren Wolfe, the marriage director at the church, blessed us with a fantastic gift basket in the room. Part of the gift was a couple's massage at the resort.

Rolling my eyes, I looked at Amy and said, "Oh great!" I was grateful for the gesture but had no need to be rubbed on for an hour while lying naked on a table. I immediately went down to the spa to trade it in for an all-day treatment for Amy. The lady at the front desk was quite the saleswoman. She said, "Do it for your wife, sir." Sure, play the guilt card. I scheduled a 4:00 massage for the next day.

After one of the most distracting morning sessions of my life, we made our way to the spa at 3:30 that afternoon. When we got there, I was led away to the men's locker room. The young lady pointed to the lockers and requested that I completely disrobe and put on the provided robe. My first thought was *That ain't gonna happen.*

The spa was filled with conference attendees. That didn't help my condition any. Fellowshiping with believers and being called "Pastor" while walking around in a robe is not something we do in the Ozarks.

We started by sipping tea in an Asian-themed cabana with our brothers and sisters in Christ. Yuck! Next, we were summoned from the hallway, alerting some ten couples from the event to the fact that the keynote speaker was only minutes away from lying naked on a table.

Once we got in the room, I took off my robe and jacket. Amy and I lay down on separate tables three feet apart. My wife was laughing the entire time. She knew every bone in my body was crying out, "Don't do this!"

Before we went in, I asked her, "Will they touch my rear end? That's all I need to know. If they are going to touch my rear end, I'm not doing the massage."

Amy said, "Just tell them not to."

Right. How in the world am I supposed to start that conversation?

Pretty soon the masseuse and masseur entered the room and began playing soft music.

My masseur, Steve, started in at my feet and figured out in the first minute that I'm ticklish. As he worked on my legs, he started digging into my thighs with his elbow. I felt a rush of pain and let out several "Oooohs," my cues for him to lighten up. Meanwhile, Amy was snickering away, having a blast with her massage, getting plenty of entertainment from mine.

He only asked me two questions during the entire massage. The first question was whether I was ticklish. I thought, *We are not going to start chitchatting right now.* His second question came while he was working on my glutes (which

Amy promised would not happen). "Are you athletic?" he asked.

What? Totally inappropriate question! I was done and ready to bolt.

Well, I survived the torturous fifty minutes. When Steve was finished, he laid my robe across my chest and whispered in my ear, "Good night."

I wanted to scream out, "Go away!"

After he left, I got up and put my robe on.

I was sitting in the fetal position at the end of the table when Amy attempted to put her arm around me. I pushed her away and muttered, "Give me a second." Never had I felt so violated.

I have regifted every massage I've ever been given. Now you know why.

I may not like being touched by strangers, but I know affection is essential to marriage and family life. Meaningful touch has physical and emotional benefits in the home. Doctors and hospitals encourage skin-to-skin contact between mother and infant as a developmental strategy for premature babies. Meaningful touch reduces stress, relieves pain, and increases life expectancy.

Your spouse needs to be touched twelve times a day. These are not to be given all at once. Spread them out throughout the day. Before you walk up to your spouse and start counting, think through the variety of touches available to you.

Your spouse needs five types of touch, and your kids need

to see four and a half of them: NSTs (nonsexual touches), STs (sexual touches), hugs, hand-holding, and kisses.

Nonsexual touching includes a hand on the shoulder as you say, "Thank you for dinner." It can also be your hand on the small of the back for a picture or an assist to a seat. How your spouse responds to NSTs communicates much to you and the kids. A relaxed, nonangry person likes to be touched. An angry person avoids touching or any kind of physical advances. NSTs can also include just standing close together. Some of my favorite times of this kind of NST are during worship at church. Amy and I sway together slightly during worship. I truly enjoy worshiping with Amy because I feel close to her.

Sexual touching includes caressing the buttock, moving your hand from under the armpit down the side to right above the hip, and just a good old-fashioned "goose" from behind. This extent of sexual touching is the half of the five touches your kids can see. I like my kids to see me appropriately flirting with their mom. Some of our spontaneous touches throughout the day are very inappropriate for our kids to witness, so we keep those to ourselves. We have only been caught on a handful of occasions. Pardon the pun.

After years of marriage, a couple was lying in bed one evening, when the wife felt her husband begin to fondle her in ways he hadn't done in quite some time. It almost tickled as his fingers started at her neck, then began moving down past the small of her back. He then caressed her shoulders and neck, slowly worked his hand down over her breasts, stopping just over her lower stomach. He then placed his hand on her left inner arm, caressed her breast again, worked down her side, passed gently over her buttock, and down her leg to her calf. Then, he proceeded up her inner thigh, stopping just at the uppermost portion of her leg. He continued in the same manner on her right side, then suddenly stopped, rolled over, and became silent.

Since she had become quite aroused by this caressing, she asked in a loving voice, "Honey, that was wonderful. Why did you stop?"

"I found the remote," he mumbled.

Sexual touching does not always mean "sex to follow." Allow this form of touching to be a fun, spontaneous break of routine.

Hugging can be nonsexual or sexual. There is the embrace that lasts longer than the hug you give Aunt Myrtle. The embrace tells your spouse that things are good and you can relax together. It also can communicate that you are not in a rush and you have nowhere else to be. Your spouse knows immediately how distracted you are by the length and intensity of the hug. I especially love it when the kids want to break up our hugs and be right in the center. Nothing says "close-knit" more than a family hug.

Hand-holding is a lost art. Most of our hand-holding is in the car and in the movie theater. There is the interlocking finger approach that requires immediate participation to work. The wrap-around-the-palm approach is most often used to test the waters after a fight. You make an initial squeeze and wait for one back. No squeeze means no forgiveness. Then you have the hand-holding thermostat to deal with. We do not hold hands for longer than five minutes due to sweaty palms. And wouldn't you know it, for the same reason Amy does not like to have our feet touch under the covers, she is the first to break it off. I am good with that because I know her temperature sensitivity. You can tell you know your lover when you both agree it is over at the same time.

Kissing has many forms. There's the "I'm sick and don't want to give you germs" air kiss. There is the "I'm feeling a cold coming on and want to be careful" peck on the cheek. It is a close cousin to the "I know you are mad at me" cheek peck. You have your good-bye and good-night kisses that always feel the same and a bit rushed. Then there is the long, passionate, deep kissing that says, "I hope tonight is the night."

Solomon says, "Your lips drop sweetness as the honeycomb, my bride; milk and honey are under your tongue" (Song of Solomon 4:11). What's he doing here? He tastes her lips and her tongue. We think of that as a French kiss, but it's a Hebrew kiss. The term *French kiss* didn't get coined until 1923, while the Hebrew kiss goes back more than three thousand years! Solomon compares the kiss, the sweetness on his love's tongue, to honey. Kissing is good for both your health and marriage.

If you want to be happy, healthy, successful, and live longer, give your spouse a kiss before you go to work each day. That's the conclusion of a study conducted by a group of

German physicians and psychologists, in cooperation with insurance companies. According to Dr. Arthur Sazbo, the study found that those who kiss their spouse each morning miss less work because of illness than those who do not. They also have fewer auto accidents on the way to work. They earn 20 to 30 percent more monthly, and they live about five years more than those who don't even give each other a peck on the cheek. The reason for this, says Dr. Sazbo, is that the kissers begin the day with a positive attitude. A kiss signifies a sort of seal of approval, offer Sazbo and his colleagues, and they believe those who don't experience it, for whatever reason, go out the door feeling not quite right about themselves.

Regular kissing is a rule in our home. No matter how hectic the morning, or if there is tension between us, we have committed to never leave in the morning without the kiss. We kiss our kids good-bye at school each morning and when we pick them up each afternoon. When we tuck Corynn in at night, she always requests that we "Eskimo kiss, kiss my nose, kiss my lips."

The Bible gives us a very descriptive term for touch in Genesis 27:26 (NASB): "Then his father Isaac said to him, 'Please come close and kiss me, my son.'" *Come close* has more than one meaning. It's the term used in Scripture for armies drawing together for battle and the intensity and the locking of arms that they need to do in order to accomplish the task ahead. It is also a Hebrew term used to describe the overlapping scales of crocodile skin, close and locked together. So when Isaac says to Jacob, "Come close to me, I want to hug you, I want to embrace you," he is grabbing his forty-year-old son. He's not giving him a gentle guy hug or a "great to see you" hug, but rather he is giving him intimate touch.

When we touch often, we pass on a blessing to our children as well as to our spouse. The more your children see you touch and bless your spouse, the more they feel touched and blessed. In Genesis 48:9, Joseph says to his father, "They are the sons God has given me here." Then Israel (Jacob) says, "Bring them to me so I may bless them." Blessing them was not just saying I'm proud of you with a hit on the arm. It was a meaningful touch that transferred a blessing (see verses 10-14).

Dr. Ross Campbell, a world-famous psychiatrist, said this, "In all of my research and in all of my own experience in counseling [his entire career], I have never known one sexually disoriented person who had a warm, loving and affectionate father." In his studies with women of the street, every one of them had a terrible relationship with her dad and was not blessed or touched meaningfully, or was abused physically.

When touch is withheld, it is damaging. When touch is withheld, so is the blessing. Touch withheld made Jesus quite angry. In Mark 10:13-14 we see Jesus' attitude toward people who would withhold touch: "People were bringing little children to Jesus to have him touch them, but the disciples rebuked them. When Jesus saw this, he was indignant." The word *indignant* can be translated as extremely angry or irate.

How many times have we seen pictures of this familiar New Testament story? I remember the flannelgraph figures from Sunday school. Jesus was sitting on a rock and smiling as the disciples gathered the little children around him. That's not the scene at all. Jesus should have a scowling look on his face. He gets on the disciples for withholding the blessing from the kids.

It's never too late to start touching. If you did not grow up in a touchy-feely home and touch is not present in your home currently, it is not too late. You will feel uncomfortable at first, but you need to let it grow on you. Bless your spouse and children with regular, meaningful touch.

Add your voice to the GPLL message . . .

Connect with us at www.greatparentslousylovers.com and watch the video podcast for chapter 16.

Post your thoughts, comments, and stories on our Web site. Here are some questions from chapter 16 to get you started on your journey to a couple-centered home:

- Did you grow up in a home with regular, meaningful touch?
- Of the five touches (NST, ST, hand-holding, kissing, and hugging), which comes naturally to you?
- Which one do you do most often?
- How do your kids respond when they see you touch your spouse?
- Which one would you like to start doing more of?
- What is your plan for flirting with your spouse in front of the kids?

TOUCHY-SUBJECT DATE:

Pick your favorite form of touch, and ask your mate to indulge you. Don't always expect your spouse to read your mind if you want a hug, a kiss, a longer kiss, sex, a massage, more foreplay, a snuggle, or even a handhold. Go ahead, ask for it!

CHAPTER 17

GREAT LOVERS

You might be a Great Parent, Lousy Lover if you have sex less than four times a month and they are all quickies.

TED... My wife cannot be romanced while camping.

Several years ago on a camping trip to Minnesota with my wife's family, we reserved a two-bedroom fishing cabin. While I enjoy spending time with family, breaking our regular routine and attempting to coordinate the schedules of twenty people can be exhausting. We had a bedroom for Corynn and a bedroom for Carson. Amy and I opted to take the pull-out couch in the cabin's main living area. The entire cabin shared a window air-conditioning unit, which kept the inside of the cabin at eighty degrees—even at ten o'clock at night. My wife is the type of woman who knows when the thermostat is set on seventy or seventy-one degrees at home.

206 II GREAT PARENTS, LOUSY LOVERS

One degree makes a difference for her. And all the women said, "Amen!"

As we lay in bed our first night, we began romancing each other—until we discovered that we could feel every spring the bed had to offer. The full-size mattress was so uncomfortable that we decided to sleep parallel to the back of the couch. With the heat, the uncomfortable bed, and the dingy floor, I knew we weren't going to be having sex anytime soon. All we could do was laugh and be thankful that the kids were comfortable.

As far as my performance, I'd give myself a C+, but that's being generous. After driving a minivan with six people in it for eleven hours, I was too tired to prepare the room—and there wasn't much of a room to prepare. Distractions were everywhere. And did I mention that the walls were paper-thin?

But do you know what? Throughout that whole week of heat, poor sleeping conditions, and family, Amy and I flirted like crazy. We had fun with it. I never laughed more about poor performance or missed opportunities in my eleven years of marriage to her. It taught us a great lesson about freedom and flexibility. We could go the week without sex and still be great. It made me anticipate the trip home. We actually cut that vacation short by a day and a half. I was less than truthful with the family as to why we were leaving. There was no way I was going to tell Amy's side of the family that I wanted to get home to have sex. (Of course, now they know.)

I'm sure you have a similar story of a time the kids and

conditions kept you and your spouse from great lovemaking. On the nights Amy and I plan on sex, it is a full-time job keeping Amy's energy in reserve. I make sure the kids do not distract her. I don't tie them up or anything like that, but I do keep them away as best I can. Think about the irony for a second. Parenting is probably the best birth control out there.

♥

In Song of Solomon 5:1 God says, "Eat, O friends, and drink; drink your fill, O lovers." The word for *drink* in the Hebrew means "to be intoxicated or to be saturated." It is the same word used for *satisfy* in Proverbs 5:18-19: "May your fountain be blessed, and may you rejoice in the wife of your youth. A loving doe, a graceful deer—may her breasts satisfy you always, may you ever be captivated by her love."

We have an entire chapter in our Bible that shows a married couple who are drunk on each other's love. It is Song of Solomon chapter 4. In the first four verses of this chapter, we see a newlywed couple, and the wife is undressing in front of her husband. Solomon shares the play-by-play.

"How beautiful you are, my darling! Oh, how beautiful! Your eyes behind your veil are doves. Your hair is like a flock of goats descending from Mount Gilead" (verse 1). Let me explain. Solomon is a king, but he is a shepherd by trade. He is using a word picture from his trade. In that day, Hebrew women pinned their hair up. His wife comes into the bridal room, takes the pin out, and her hair falls down around her shoulders. All he can picture is being out with the flock and seeing, from Mount Gilead, these goats coming down the mountainside. So she has now dropped her hair.

Verse 2 says, "Your teeth are like a flock of sheep just shorn, coming up from the washing. Each has its twin; not one of them is alone." They are clean, they are straight, and she has them all. That is awesome. I don't know what else you'd want from your wife's teeth than for them to be clean and straight and all there. He can see her teeth because his bride is smiling while she undresses. This once-insecure young lady is now secure as she undresses before her new husband.

She is smiling at him as she undresses, and this is pretty significant because in the first chapter of the book she tells Solomon not to stare at her. "Dark am I, yet lovely . . . dark like the tents of Kedar, like the tent curtains of Solomon. . . . Do not stare at me because I am dark, because I am darkened by the sun. My mother's sons were angry with me and made me take care of the vineyards; my own vineyard [speaking of her body] I have neglected" (verses 5-6). In that day, paleness was beauty, not a suntan. They didn't go down to their local gas station and get into a tanning bed like we do here in the Ozarks. So in chapter 1, she addresses the two primary insecurities of women: family history and their bodies.

Solomon comes in as a shepherd-king stud and says, honey, you are like a horse (verse 9). Let us explain. He says like a mare harnessed to one of Pharaoh's chariots. In that day, when Pharaoh showed up on the battlefield, he was surrounded by chariots all pulled by dark horses. But the one horse that pulled his chariot was white. It was a white mare. He is saying that you stand out above all of those. He immediately speaks to her insecurities. Guys, what a lesson for us. Care for the insecurities of our wives, and help build safety and security into not just the marriage but into the bedroom. And remember, if your wife ever asks, "Do these jeans make my butt look big?" be careful. There is only one answer to that question. And the right answer will build security into your marriage and bedroom.

Song of Solomon 4:3 says, "Your lips are like a scarlet ribbon; your mouth is lovely. Your temples behind your veil are like the halves of a pomegranate." This means they are red and there is blood going through her cheeks. Verse 4 goes on to say, "Your neck is like the tower of David, built with elegance; on it hang a thousand shields, all of them shields of warriors." Solomon is speaking here of nobility. She is not sitting down as a sheepish bride; she is looking at him with security and boldness.

Ladies, one of the best gifts you can give your husband is to undress slowly in front of him. Undressing is very sexual and a huge turn-on for guys. Don't rush. If you are insecure about your body, turn off the lights and light a votive in the far corner of the room and make him squint.

Verse 5 addresses the issue of gentleness: "Your two breasts are like two fawns, like twin fawns of a gazelle that browse among the lilies." Why gentleness? If you want to see the fawns, you don't come running up to them, screaming and yelling. You are gentle. This is why young grooms shouldn't come out packing heat like Walker, Texas Ranger, on their honeymoon. Pastor Tommy Nelson in Denton, Texas, says, "Guys, on your honeymoon, don't come swinging out of the bathroom like Conan the Barbarian."

To be a great lover to your wife, be gentle. Men do not desire gentleness, but they do desire responsiveness from their wives. A quiet wife in the bedroom is not what the husband is looking for. He wants to know he is pleasing you, that you are enjoying it. When you have an orgasm, he wants to know. He does not want to get to the end of lovemaking and go, "Oh, I'm sorry you didn't get there," only to have you say you did.

"You did? How come you didn't let me know! I was thinking about everything from the State of the Union address to barbequing, keeping my mind on something else." Most men can be done at a moment's notice; you just have to let us know.

Do you know what Beth Moore says? She was discipled early in her marriage by an older woman who taught her never to let her hands stop moving.

"Until the day breaks and the shadows flee, I will go to the mountain of myrrh and to the hill of incense" (verse 6). In this verse Solomon is saying that he wants to be intoxicated by her touch all night long. One of the best questions we've ever been asked on sex is how often should an evangelical couple have sex. We love that. As opposed to other world religions? We have no idea, but we encourage two to three times a week. We actually tell couples getting married that if they are not planning on having sex two to three times per week, then they don't need to get married. It's about intimacy, not just frequency, but there is something to be said for consistently connecting with each other.

TED... Can I give some tips for those who say you always have good intentions, but the kids keep you from sex on most nights?

First, guys, the most important equation for understanding sex and your wife is this: energy = sex drive. To be ready at night, your wife needs to reserve energy during the day. That's why Gary Smalley says men are microwaves and women are Crock-Pots. Women turn on early in the morning and they start cooking all day long. Then they are ready to enjoy the night. Men are microwaves, ready in a minute and sometimes done in a minute. Many guys expect their wives to turn on like a microwave at night, and they go at it for an hour even though she's absolutely exhausted. So you have to think earlier in the day about what you can do to help her conserve energy.

Second, two very important words help your wife conserve energy: domestic support. It's called chores in our home. Doing the dishes is preparing your wife for sex. When you vacuum, it's turning her on. When you take care of the kids, she is getting in the mood. Get it? Ted Cunningham wrestling or fighting in the family room with Carson . . . "Let's do battle, Dad."

Third, learn to enjoy the quickie. For Meryl and Anthony,

the only way they could pull off a Sunday-afternoon quickie was to send their eight-year-old son out on the balcony with a Popsicle and tell him to report on all the neighborhood activities.

While in bed, the couple could hear their son announcing, "There's a car being towed down the street."

A few moments later he shouted, "An ambulance just drove by!"

"Looks like the Andersons have company," he called out.

"Matt's riding a new bike!" he declared with a trace of envy.

"Looks like the Sanders are moving," he proclaimed.

"Jason is on his skateboard," he yelled.

"The Coopers are having sex!" he announced confidently.

Startled, Meryl and Anthony jumped out of bed. Anthony called out, "Son, how do you know they're having sex?"

"Because Jimmy Cooper is standing on his balcony with a Popsicle too."

Let's face it, even the quickie isn't easy if you have children. But a quickie can go a long way to spicing up your sex life. One of the best tips I ever heard on quickies is something Steve Doocy taught me in his book *The Mr. and Mrs. Happy Handbook: Everything I Know About Love and Marriage (with corrections by Mrs. Doocy)*. If you want to pull off a quickie in the middle of the afternoon with preschoolers, place two sets of shoes in the dryer and set it for thirty minutes. Two important things happen: 1) You have a timer—most men won't need a half hour, but it's there just in case; 2) The dryer becomes the loudest activity in the house.

———— 🖤 ————

Now let's move on to affirmation. Song of Solomon 4:7 says, "All beautiful you are, my darling; there is no flaw in you." This is what every woman wants to hear because she is insecure about family and she's insecure about body image issues. She wants to hear and be affirmed that there is no flaw in her. Once the Shulamite woman exposes her naked body to Solomon, he says, "You are perfect." Perfection has nothing to do with diets, surgeries, nips, tucks, or skin. "No flaw" is the battle cry of a man who has saved his affection for one woman, his wife. He compares her to no one else. She is his!

Then he goes even further into this whole security and safety thing. Verse 8 says, "Come with me from Lebanon, my bride, come with me from Lebanon. Descend from the crest of Amana, from the top of Senir, the summit of Hermon, from the lions' dens and the mountain haunts of the leopards." He is saying she will be safe with him. He will be a gentle lover and allow her to create the boundaries in the bedroom. At the end of this chapter we will give you an unbelievable tool to help you on this journey toward emotional security and safety between spouses.

Every marriage needs vigilant protection to guard against affairs. In the blink of an eye, the trust and security that are the foundation of a healthy marriage can be destroyed, and it takes years of dedicated work to rebuild that trust. But there are steps you can take to protect your relationship.

To protect your marriage, you need to guard the marriage bed. Guys, we need to protect our wives in the bedroom and guard our hearts from sexual temptation. Make a commitment to grow closer to your wife. Be aware of your thoughts and choices every day. Draw a clear line of what you won't do, and then stay far away from it. For each person, the safety line may be a little different, but no matter who you are, you need to become accountable to someone. Everyone needs someone other than a spouse who can ask the difficult questions such as, "Did you compromise your standards last week?" or "Have you been getting your emotional needs met from someone other than your mate?" Do whatever it takes to guard your marriage, your mate, and your bedroom.

"You have stolen my heart, my sister, my bride; you have stolen my heart with one glance of your eyes, with one jewel of your necklace. How delightful is your love, my sister, my bride! How much more pleasing is your love than wine, and the fragrance of your perfume than any spice!" (verses 9-10). Solomon continues building that security. When you go back to Song of Solomon 1:17, it says, "The beams of our house are cedars; our rafters are firs," meaning we live in a mansion of security. Guys, he's brought that security into the bedroom.

We've gotten pretty hot and steamy so far in the book. Now look what happens. They're going to kiss. Wow, kissing is a part of sexual intimacy. Song of Solomon 4:11 says, "Your lips drop sweetness as the honeycomb, my bride; milk and honey are under your tongue. The fragrance of your garments is like that of Lebanon." The Hebrew kiss outdates the French kiss by some thirteen hundred years. They are enjoying a deep, sensual kiss.

In verses 12-14 we get into something that is—repeat this word after me—*foreplay.* "You are a garden locked up, my sister, my bride; you are a spring enclosed, a sealed fountain. Your plants are an orchard of pomegranates with choice fruits, with henna and nard, nard and saffron, calamus and cinnamon, with every kind of incense tree, with myrrh and aloes and all the finest spices."

Then he says this: "You are a garden fountain." Now look at the switch there from verse 12 to verse 15. Before marriage, you are a garden locked up. It's a great image. This is a very graphic image in verse 15. This isn't just some flowery language. Because he has now prepared her, she is a well of flowing water streaming down from Lebanon. Women produce a natural vaginal lubrication. We believe clearly and commentators say that's exactly what is happening here. She is prepared sexually to be with her husband.

Here's what I love about this chapter in the Song of Solomon: The reader is not present for the lovemaking. The act of intercourse is between husband, wife, and God only. "Awake, north wind, and come, south wind!" (verse 16). She is saying she wants him to be strong but gentle. One wind was a strong wind and one wind was a gentle wind.

"Blow on my garden, that its fragrance may spread abroad" (verse 16).

Then they make love.

In the next chapter they are lying back and Solomon says, "I have come into my garden, my sister, my bride; I have gathered my myrrh with my spice. I have eaten my honeycomb and my honey; I have drunk my wine and my milk" (5:1).

Then God speaks. "Eat, O friends, and drink; drink your fill, O lovers" (5:1). He's saying, *I want you to enjoy this. I have given this to you as a gift.*

Great sex flows from a great marriage.

Add your voice to the GPLL message . . .

Connect with us at www.greatparentslousylovers.com and watch the video podcast for chapter 17.

Post your thoughts, comments, and stories on our Web site. Listed below are fifty questions to get you started on your journey to a couple-centered home:

COUPLE QUESTIONS

Appetizers (Safe Questions)

- How often, if ever, did you and your parents talk about sex?
- What kind of picture did your parents paint for you about sex?
- When and where did you first learn about sex?
- Is sex an embarrassing subject for you?

- Are there any questions about sex that you think are off-limits for us to discuss?

- Give an example of an off-limits question.

- What parts of your body are you insecure about? What can I do to ease those insecurities?

- Do you like it when I undress in front of you? Should I slow it down?

- Do you like what I wear leading up to sex (i.e., should I burn the sweats)?

- What would you change about our bedroom to spice it up?

Frequency

- On a scale of 1 to 10, how satisfied are you with how often we have sex?

- I enjoy having sex ___ times per week or month.

- How often do you reach climax/orgasm when we make love?

- Have you ever been frustrated thinking, *Tonight's the night,* only to be disappointed? Does this happen often?

- What time of day is the best time for you?

- What should our code words be around the kids on the night we are in the mood? (E.g., "working on the budget" or "Do we need anything at the supermarket?" Nobody uses the word *supermarket* anymore, so that works.)

- Do we do well sharing the initiation?

- Do we offer grace to each other when "tonight's the night" doesn't work out? Do we ever show anger?

Performance

- On a scale of 1 to 10, how satisfied are you with our performance?
- What can we do to bring our sex life out of a rut?
- Can you give me two or three ideas for foreplay?
- Do I move through foreplay too quickly? Or is it too much time?
- What gets you in the mood more than anything?
- What are some practical ways we can prepare the bedroom for lovemaking?
- What position is most comfortable for you?
- Do you prefer to be on top or on bottom?
- Should we sleep nude more often?
- Should we shower together?
- Am I too rough when I kiss or massage your breasts?
- Is there anything I ever do that makes you uncomfortable or causes you pain?
- What sounds do you like hearing to know that I am enjoying it?
- Should we use more candles?
- What genre of music would you want on our lovemaking playlist?
- Lotions, oils, scents? You in?
- I like it best when you . . . (after a few years the list is five pages long).
- It makes me uncomfortable when you . . .

- What are the distractions that keep us from getting together?
- Are you interested in me rubbing or lightly massaging your clitoris?
- You good with outside?
- Is oral sex okay with you? What can we do to be more creative?
- Who sets the boundaries for creativity?

Endurance

- On a scale of 1 to 10, how satisfied are you with how long we spend making love?
- Do you ever feel like we rush it?
- On the days when life is crazy and when it has been a while since we have been intimate, are you good with quickies?
- What concerns do you have about quickies?
- How long should sex last?
- Have you ever been frustrated at how long it takes me to get in the mood?
- Have you ever been frustrated at how long it takes me to reach climax?
- How can I gain ejaculatory control?
- Is getting there at the same time important?

TURN-UP-THE-HEAT DATE:

It's your turn to add a fresh spark to bedtime. If you don't usually bother with candles, take time to set up a few. Try massage oil or a shower for two. Women, revisit that long-forgotten lingerie store for something new and sexy—and actually wear it. Men, buy her something new, and assure her that she's still hot.

CHAPTER 18

SEX AFTER KIDS

You might be a Great Parent, Lousy Lover if your "Tonight's the night" is regularly met with "Let's shoot for tomorrow night."

TED… Corynn's birth was one of the single most important days of our marriage and lives. She was born around eight-thirty in the morning on August 4, 2003. My wife was a trooper. I knew she was a strong woman, but her stock shot way up in my book after watching her battle through labor for nine hours. There were no complications, and I was giving Corynn her first bath by nine-thirty.

During bath time Amy was tended to by the nursing staff and was moved from the birthing room to a regular room down the hall. The nurses on that first shift were amazing. Sweet and kind, they were over-the-top gracious in their care for Mommy, baby, and even Daddy.

The regular tests were performed on Corynn throughout the day, but other than that, she spent most of the day in the room with us greeting family and friends. As nighttime came around, we were greeted by the second shift of nurses. Again, they were sweet and over-the-top friendly. But there was one nurse I will never forget.

She was passionate about nursing and had been in the field for at least three decades. Eligible for retirement, she was the type to keep working another three decades. She was strong, to the point, and more blunt than anyone else I had ever met in the medical field. She had much to say to Amy and only one line to say to me.

To Amy she spoke like a coach calling plays, "Now, honey, you need to get some good rest tonight and let us take care of the baby. She'll be fine. You did great today, and you're going to recover, no problem. I'll check in on you throughout the night. You just press this button if you need anything. And I mean anything."

Then she turned to me and delivered one of the most shocking statements I have ever received: "And for you, there will be no sex going on in this room tonight."

What? No words came out of my mouth, but she could tell from my wide-eyed, jaw-dropped expression that I was floored.

So she continued, "Son, I have walked in on more guys making advances on their wives after childbirth, getting all fresh and wanting some. I break it up immediately."

I would not believe such a thing if I read it in a book, but this nurse was quite convincing. I had spent much of the day watching Amy struggle in pain from the bed to the sink and back to the bed and could not imagine making an advance. Also, I knew the rule was a six-week sexual Sabbath. The doctor hadn't instructed me yet, but I knew it was coming.

"Ma'am, I can promise you that it was not even in my mind," I assured her.

"Good," she said, "but I don't take anything for granted, and I give that warning to every young husband."

How sick does a person have to be to do something like that? Just her bringing it up to me made me feel dirty.

The next night the same nurse wheeled in a cart with a television and VCR and one instruction: "We need you to watch this shaken-baby-syndrome video before you leave the hospital tomorrow."

Not thinking, I said, "Oh, that won't be a problem; we don't need to watch it." Wrong thing to say.

"It is guys just like you who shake babies," she snapped at me.

Not only was I a pervert in her book, but I was also an abusive father. Seven years later, her words still haunt me at night.

We did wait the six weeks, but even after that sabbatical, sex was a real struggle. New parents face many challenges and distractions, and keeping the romance alive takes work. It may not be as spontaneous as it was before kids, but it can be just as enjoyable. Actually, we have found that sex after kids is even better.

♥

Here are some very practical steps you can take to have hot, passionate sex after the kids come along.

First, be okay with appointment sex. It is not all that sexy. Some find it demeaning. Others find it necessary. Since sexual interest builds, it sometimes can be the first step toward renewed passion. You can probably share stories of times when you weren't in the mood, but after you got started, you got in the mood. There have been plenty of days in our marriage when neither Amy nor I were in the mood. Yes, even as a guy I have those days when sex feels like too much work. Long hours at work, sick kids, all-day baseball tournaments with your kids in ninety-degree heat, and even camping can hinder the lovin' feelin'. It is on those nights that Amy and I look at each other while brushing our teeth and say, "You know, it has been a long week." It surprises both of us how quickly we get in the mood after we get started. Setting times and places in advance is not a bad thing. Just be cautious to not allow appointment sex to become routine.

Second, remove distractions. Making love next to a baby monitor is sort of like making love next to a car alarm ready to go off. It puts you a smidge on edge. Guys can have distracted sex. We can work through it. While most women need to focus on the act to reach orgasm, a husband usually needs to focus on something else to keep from orgasm. Amazing how that works.

Here are just a few ways to remove distractions before sex:

1. Brush off crumbs in bed left there by children during their afternoon snack.
2. Throw away dirty diapers and anything related to the changing of a baby.
3. Move the dinner dishes from the sink to the dishwasher.
4. Stuff clutter from dresser tops into drawers.
5. Make the bed even if it has been unmade all day. Fresh is good.
6. Make sure the door is locked. Security is important.
7. Turn on a white noise machine or radio.
8. Make sure small children have gone potty, had a good meal, and have gotten a sip of water.

TED... That last one is key. You need to know that the kids are sleeping well. As a young husband and father, I had no idea how much of a distraction a sleeping child was for my wife. Sex after feedings instead of right before them made for better sex. The thought of Corynn waking up and needing something was always in the back of Amy's mind.

Third, conserve energy for sex. It might sound counterintuitive, but one of the best ways to make sure you have energy is to exercise regularly. The only thing that gets me through the winter and my seasonal affective disorder is exercise. We can easily mistake all of the running around with the kids as exercise. It is not. Busyness and exercise are mutually exclusive. Even with your full calendar, be sure to schedule in time to be healthy and active and to eat right.

TED… My friend Mark Connelly is a fitness fanatic. When we launched a new ministry for couples, he insisted that one of the main messages focus on getting fit as a couple. I resisted at first. There was a lot of back-and-forth between us, but ultimately we added it to our messages. He pointed to 1 Corinthians 7:4 as his main argument for couples being healthy together: "The wife's body does not belong to her alone but also to her husband." Amen on that one, right? The verse continues, "In the same way, the husband's body does not belong to him alone but also to his wife."

Husbands, we are supposed to care about ourselves and our responsibilities, and wives should care about themselves and their responsibilities. My responsibility as Amy's husband is to offer my best to her—heart, soul, mind, and strength. Bringing my best to her physically does make a difference in our marriage.

The American Heart Association estimates that there are a quarter million deaths per year in the United States that are directly attributed to lack of regular exercise. That is 12 percent of the total number of deaths. Each year 250,000 people die because of laziness.

If I don't care for myself physically and I die prematurely and my wife becomes a widow prematurely, then she has to suffer because I didn't bring my best physically to the marriage. That isn't what I want for her. I want her to have my best for as long as God keeps me here. I want to extend the number of days of our marriage as long as I possibly can.

Not only does physical health have the obvious effect of allowing us to be with our loved ones, but it also impacts our whole-being interconnectedness—bodies, emotions, energy . . . everything. Physical vitality affects our entire marriage.

A study at the Mayo Clinic argues for the benefits of regular exercise: "Exercise improves your mood. . . . Physical activity stimulates brain chemicals that may leave you feeling happier and more relaxed . . . and even help prevent depression. . . . A good night's sleep improves concentration, productivity and mood. . . . Regular physical activity can help you fall asleep faster and deepen your sleep."[1] Regular exercise and good sleep and eating right go a long way toward making you a nicer person to be around.

Another benefit is that exercise brings more energy to your marriage. The Mayo Clinic report also says that exercise boosts your energy level. Physical activity delivers oxygen and nutrients to your tissues, which helps your entire cardio-vascular system. When your heart and lungs work more efficiently, you have more energy to do the things you enjoy. In other words, when you are exercising and you're feeling better and your body is healthier, it doesn't have to work so hard, leaving you more energy to spare.

The Mayo Clinic report says exercise affects your sex life. Regular physical activity often leads to enhanced arousal for women and reduces the risk of erectile dysfunction in men.

When you take care of yourself physically, you have more

confidence in the bedroom. You don't feel like hiding with the lights out. Because of the interconnectedness of our bodies, souls, and emotions, physical health adds to the joy God wants you to have in the bedroom.

Taking care of ourselves is nothing to kid around about. It really is important to bring our best to our spouses in all of who God made us to be.

Mark Connelly has had a major influence on Amy and me. We exercise together as a couple a minimum of three times a week. I love running alongside her on the treadmill. We have noticed a big shift in our energy levels, especially during the dark, cold days of winter. It has given us more energy for our work, kids, and each other.

--------- ♥ ---------

In the last chapter we looked at Song of Solomon 4. This young couple enjoyed great sex together. Then, according to one interpretation, no sooner did they get home from the honeymoon, they had a fight over sex. In Song of Solomon 5:2, the young bride says, "I slept but my heart [Solomon] was awake. Listen! My lover is knocking: 'Open to me, my sister, my darling, my dove, my flawless one.'"

Solomon initiates sex with his young bride. His bride continues to respond in verse 3: "I have taken off my robe—must I put it on again? I have washed my feet—must I soil them again?" My paraphrase: "I'm not in the mood." We all have times when we are not in the mood. And that is okay. We do not need to condemn each other when that happens.

When your lover is not in the mood, respond as Solomon did. Verses 4-5 say, "My lover thrust his hand through the latch-opening; my heart began to pound for him. I arose to open for my lover, and my hands dripped with myrrh." Solomon reached through the door and offered liquid myrrh, which is a sign of sweetness. He did not judge, condemn, or taunt her. He walked away peacefully.

His response caused his bride to respond. His response aroused his wife. Verse 6 says, "I opened for my lover, but my lover had left; he was gone. My heart sank at his departure. I looked for him but did not find him. I called him but he did not answer."

Maybe you often are not in the mood and you constantly hear, "You always use the 'I'm tired' excuse" or "We haven't had any in weeks." Remember your commitment. Sex is a key part of marriage. So remember your commitment: You no longer own your body. Husbands and wives are to honor and adore each other.

Add your voice to the GPLL message . . .

Connect with us at www.greatparentslousylovers.com and watch the video podcast for chapter 18.

Post your thoughts, comments, and stories on our Web site. Here are some questions from chapter 18 to get you started on your journey to a couple-centered home:

- How do you feel about appointment sex?

- Name a few distractions that your spouse could help remove.
- Are you taking care of yourself physically? Do you have a healthy diet? Are you exercising?
- What are your common excuses to keep you from being fit for your spouse?
- What helps you conserve energy throughout the day?
- What steps can you take to feel more attractive if that's an area of struggle for you? How can you encourage your spouse that he or she is beautiful to you?

DINNER AND A MOVING:

Get that blood moving. Make a date for eating healthy. Cook your own meal or eat out with the goal of choosing something healthy from the menu. Then take a walk or bike ride together. Make it an early date, if possible, so you can enjoy a good night's sleep. Here's to lots of healthy years together!

CHAPTER 19

GREAT MEN, GREAT WOMEN

You might be a Great Parent, Lousy Lover if you've ever wondered why your spouse wasn't just like you.

TED… The differences between men and women are obvious at birth and play out relationally early in life. My daughter is a kindergartner and believes that most boys in her class are troublemakers. I get the privilege of picking her up from school every day, and the story is always the same.

"Dad, the boys were not good again today," she says and then rattles off the name of each boy who had to turn over his card. A turned-over card is the first warning toward a time-out.

"Oh yeah, what did they do?" I inquire.

"They are always talking and playing rough with each

other," she says. I usually shake my head because I think I have a pretty good idea of what is going on.

I have visited Corynn's classroom on several occasions for lunch, reading time, and writing class. What I observe in the boys is not troublemaking, but rather something even more disturbing: They are acting like little boys.

Let me give you an example. During one visit to reading time the teacher was reading a book on snowball fights. She inquired of the class, "How many of you had a snowball fight last week during Christmas break?" Several of the girls raised their hands. Not the boys. They had to act out the snowball fight. They had to show the teacher what a snowball fight looked like. They were being boys.

Here is my observation. Boys will make it through the schools a lot easier the sooner they conform to femininity. Now before you send me an angry e-mail, hear me out. Wait until the end of the chapter before you throw stones.

We live in a culture that wants to blur the lines of Genesis 1:27: "God created man in his own image, in the image of God he created him; male and female he created them." I have never conducted an official study, but if I did, I'm sure it would conclude that men make bad women and women make bad men. We are equal but different. Little girls need to act like little girls, and little boys need to act like little boys.

There are two systems of thought when it comes to discussing the differences between men and women. First, there is the egalitarian system. It teaches that men and women are equal on all levels. Minimize the differences between them and do not assign roles. Husband and wife both lead in the home and church. The key verse used by egalitarians is Ephesians 5:21: "Submit to one another out of reverence for Christ."

Second, there is the complementarian system. This system teaches that men and women are equal in value, but different in roles. I am a complementarian. I'm not so extreme as to believe that women can't lead or be CEOs of companies, as some complementarians teach. I will admit that I grew up in the complementarian system. I went to a seminary and a college that was complementarian. The cool part is that I have dear friends who are egalitarians. We can enjoy meals together and get along well. So there's no need to write me an e-mail.

I want my daughter to grow up enjoying being a woman. I want my son to enjoy being a man.

God stamped his image and character on both masculinity and femininity. Author John Eldredge covered this topic in his book *Wild at Heart* when he asked the question "Where have all the good men gone?" Where are they? Why are they giving up in the home and in their marriages? Why are they giving up on the church?

I believe that the church and school have neutered men. We have tried to turn all the men into women. That's the problem.

Last year Carson had his turn for show-and-tell at his preschool. Toy weapons are banned from the school, which left my son with very few objects to show. The best he could come up with was a few G.I. Joes. They had weapons, but they were small enough to go undetected.

It just so happened to be my helper day at his school, so I got to be there for his presentation. As he sat on the chair in front of the class, hitting the two men against each other, he said, "These are my army men, and they love to fight each other!"

"Oh my, Carson," the teacher said gently, "are there any other toys you have at home that you would like to tell us about?"

Carson's answer was priceless: "Guns and knives." That was one of the proudest moments of my life.

You may be asking, "Ted, are you raising violent children?" Nope, I'm raising a boy!

Modern Christianity and the church have mothered our men to death. The church has portrayed one side of God and left out the other mighty warrior side of God who instructed his chosen people to attack his enemies.

When raising boys, the recipe is simple for fun. To any activity, add an element of danger, exploration, or destruction, and you've got a winner. That's boys, and I don't ever want to change that. I want Carson to grow up and be a man.

Every little girl and every little boy asks one fundamental question, but it is often very different between the sexes. Little boys want to know this: "Do I have what it takes?" All that rough-and-tumble and daring and superhero stuff is boys seeking to prove that they have what it takes, that they can do it. "I can fly off the top of this couch in my cape, Dad.

It will work; I know it will. . . . Dad, I can jump off the roof and I'll be all right. . . ." You'll see a lot more YouTube video clips of boys jumping off the second story balcony into the swimming pool. Sure, some girls are adventurous, too, but boys tend to have that burning desire to prove themselves. Men are fueled by that search for validation to their question, "Do I have what it takes?"

Last summer, Gary and I were with Dr. Dobson in Colorado Springs. After our radio interview, Dr. Dobson pulled me aside and asked me about Carson: "You have a son, right, Ted?"

"Yes sir, Dr. Dobson, and he is all boy," I answered.

"Do you two play rough with each other?" he asked.

"Yeah, we mess around and play fight almost every day." I responded with one raised eyebrow because I could tell he was leading me somewhere.

"No, Ted, I mean do you let Carson whale on you like little boys should do with their dads?" he insisted.

Knowing there is only one way to answer the world's expert on parenting, I responded with a slight rasp in my voice, "I will from now on."

"You let him kick and hit at you and get that little aggression out. And don't stop until he is tired. Don't stop even if your wife is in the kitchen telling you to be careful or to stop before someone gets hurt," he said.

That little corner conversation in the studio has permanently changed our home. Each night I am greeted at the door by my precious Corynn with a smile and a picture. "Do you like this picture I drew of our family, Daddy? I put this smiling sun up in this corner because it is a beautiful day and we are all happy," she shares while giving me a hug.

As I turn to face Carson, he yells out, "Do you want a piece of me?"

"You ready for battle, my mighty warrior?" I ask.

"Let's fight in the living room, Dad," he demands.

"Go easy on me, Carson; it's been a tough day."

Yet he shows no mercy. He initiates the battle by raising his fists and declaring, "You mess with the bull, you get the horns!"

My wife says our battles are some of her favorite times of day. They get out some of his testosterone, which means he treats his sister and mommy in a more gentle way. Since Dr. Dobson's private tutorial with me, Amy has seen an amazing change in Carson. He knows that these battles are only with Daddy and not with Mommy and Sissy. Mommy is the queen, and Sissy is the princess. Carson will often take a break from our battles to run over and give his mommy a kiss. Then it is back to the couch for a flying leap, knee in my ribs. He's all boy! I would have it no other way.

Little girls ask a very different question. They ask, "Am I lovely?" Solomon answered that question perfectly by telling the Shulamite bride, "All beautiful you are, my darling; there is no flaw in you" (Song of Solomon 4:7). Every little girl needs to hear from her dad and mom, "God gave you your body, and you are beautiful."

Women have been uniquely gifted by God with an innate

desire for great relationships. Unlike most men, women tend to be great at expressing their emotions. Not only can most women express how they are feeling, but they can also survey a room and share what the others in the room are feeling. Norma Smalley calls this "reading their spirit." Women can sense and feel the emotions of others.

It is a rare sight to witness one man asking another man, "How are you feeling today?" We always assume everything is fine. Many men find it difficult to discuss things that have to do with relationships or feelings. A woman may ask, "How do you feel about your work?" The man will be tempted to offer the standard response, "I feel fine." The reason? Many men aren't comfortable talking about their feelings and don't know how to respond. Women are great at understanding. Men approach everything with a duct-tape mentality. If we think we can fix it, we'll jump in and offer solutions.

Every brain starts out female. Between five and seven weeks in the womb, a testosterone drip starts. That drip destroys all the connectors between the left and right sides of the brain. In other words, brain damage occurs early. It makes men process in a compartmentalized manner. Our minds go to one room and shut the door, then they go into another room and shut the door, and so on. We discuss one issue at a time. We must complete one conversation before starting another. We are not great at multitasking.

Women are more like a river. They flow. The past, present, and the future all flow together. They remember details. Women experience and process life with both sides of their brains, logically as well as emotionally. When people's experiences touch their emotions, the experiences are easier to remember. For instance, students who study information using their right brain and feelings tend to remember the information for a longer period of time and in greater detail.

Sometimes a man will come home from work, and the wife will ask, "Did you think about me today?" The man will respond, "Well, let me think. I'm sure I did." Generally, men tend to compartmentalize. When they're at work, they're at work; when they're at home, they're at home.

When Amy and I are driving down the road, she occasionally glances over at me and asks, "What are you thinking about right now?" This always catches me off guard. She has a hard time believing that men can park their brains in neutral and be thinking about absolutely nothing. I usually find something quick to say: "We need an oil change in four hundred miles." (That little sticker in the upper left-hand corner of the windshield was the first thing I saw.) Ladies, let me share with you an important fact: If you are ever wondering whether or not your husband is thinking about the relationship, he's likely not.

Women are deeply connected to their environment. Men can detach from their surroundings. For many women, the home is an extension of who they are, and the little details can make a big difference when it comes to their comfort level.

Have you ever been headed out the door and heard your

wife say, "Oh, I forgot to wash the dishes" or "I didn't make the bed"? It's really hard for a woman to just walk out when things are undone. It's almost as if a part of her is undone. I can leave the house without worrying about the dishes, but she can't. When I understand this difference, I am better equipped to love and serve her in a way that makes her feel comfortable and more secure in our relationship and home.

When women try to answer the question "Am I lovely?" independent of God, they go in two extreme directions. One direction, they will tend to be dominating and controlling. The other, they will become too vulnerable. In fourteen years of church ministry I have seen much frustration fueled by these two extremes. A lady who wants to get her husband to church . . . a lady who wants her husband to lead . . . I've heard it time and time again in this church.

Domineering women want to control, and needy women make themselves vulnerable. Most television shows depict one of these two extremes. Both are answering the question "Am I lovely?" improperly.

Every man fears failure. That's why over and over again in Scripture you see God looking at the guys and saying, "Hey boys, don't be afraid. I'm going to go there with you. I've already set up the battlefield for the battle you are preparing to face. Don't be afraid. Don't be scared. Go and do it. I know the outcome. I've already prepared the enemy. You can't see it now, but please don't be afraid." That's my paraphrase of what Moses reported from God in Exodus 14:13.

For some, there's a battle before you and you know it,

but you won't face it because of fear. Some of you won't take the next step in your spiritual journey because of fear. Some of you won't begin leading in your homes and in the church because of fear. I would have gotten out of ministry a long time ago if failure was a disqualifier.

There is a battle before you guys that you must win and win decisively. In the back of your mind you are wondering . . .

What if I don't have what it takes to win this battle?

What if I'm not good enough?

What if I'm not strong enough?

I can't afford another false start.

I've tried before and I have failed.

Can I actually win this battle?

Great Dads and Husbands

This fear of failure in men can lead to passivity. And the passivity of Dad kills the home.

A major difference exists between the observing dad and the engaged dad. I was really convicted while writing this book about being an engaged dad rather than an observing dad. It's very easy for me to slip into observation mode, to watch Amy with the kids, to let the kids work it out themselves when they are fighting.

As a husband and a dad, I must engage my home. I must be involved. It's what being the spiritual leader means. Beware of the trap of observing. I must engage my home by leading my home in discipline and making spiritual decisions.

Dads, when we go passive, we put too much on Mom. Our passivity drains the home of energy; it drains the home of discipline; it drains the home of longevity. My engagement at home takes a burden off Amy. I don't mind being heavy with discipline. I don't mind being heavy with discipline to relieve her of that responsibility by herself.

Great Moms and Wives

Because women tend to be in touch with emotions—theirs and others'—they can tend to struggle with feelings of guilt. Am I giving my kids enough of me? Am I too hard on them? I can't seem to get through to this kid! I feel guilty for having so little time and energy for my husband.

When you allow guilt trips about parenting to creep into your home, they weigh on you emotionally to the point your husband feels disrespected. It is not intentional on your part. The little bird making the most noise gets the worm. Most men will not compete for attention. Instead, they will go passive.

Disrespect and guilt can destroy the home. Your kids will send you on a regular guilt trip if you let them. A weekend getaway with your husband leaves the kids crying at times, and that is okay. They will survive. They will be better off for it.

We've talked about saying no to activities and events in this book. Your spouse needs you to say no to the kids from time to time.

"Mommy, will you do crafts with me?"

"No, I am going to sit in the living room and talk to Daddy for a few minutes."

"Mommy, I need a juice box."

"Not right now."

"Mommy, can we stay up late tonight?"

"No, Dad and I need some alone time."

Now, there are times when saying yes works in your favor. Amy and I really enjoy our candlelight dinners at night when the kids are at home. We set the table, prepare the meal, pour the drinks, and start eating thirty minutes early, without the kids. We then invite them to the table to join us. They are usually done pretty quickly and ask to be excused.

"Absolutely, yes!" we say in unison and enjoy another thirty minutes together sipping our coffee and talking.

It can be very romantic until we hear Carson yell from the bathroom down the hall, "Momma, can you help me wipe?" That gets an immediate yes.

Celebrate your spouse—and your differences. Your marriage will be the richer for it.

Add your voice to the GPLL message . . .

Connect with us at www.greatparentslousylovers.com and watch the video podcast for chapter 19.

Post your thoughts, comments, and stories on our Web site. Here are some questions from chapter 19 to get you started on your journey to a couple-centered home:

- Name a few differences between men and women that are fun to celebrate.
- Why do you think people want to blur the lines of God's created distinction between male and female?
- What is the greatest, most celebrated difference between you and your spouse?
- Dad, how can you better engage at home?
- Mom, how can you celebrate your husband, free from guilt with the kids?

HOW-SWEET-IT-IS DATE:

Why did you marry your mate? What qualities drew you in and got your heart beating wildly? What was it that convinced you about the one you committed your life to? Each day this week, leave a note for your spouse explaining one reason you're glad you married him or her.

CHAPTER 20

GREAT CHURCHES, GREAT MARRIAGES

You might be a Great Parent, Lousy Lover if you choose a church based only on its kickin' kids program.

GARY… Our children must know that God wants their mom and dad to be husband and wife for life. We must elevate marriage ministry with parenting ministry. One thing I appreciate about my pastor and coauthor is his strong desire to add a marriage strand to our DNA at Woodland Hills. I am convinced this is the next step for the church.

Revolutionary Idea #1—The local church is a main igniter for marriage. (See Hebrews 13:4.)

I remember being at my church in Waco and feeling the call of God on my life for marriage ministry. The church responded well to my calling by blessing and sending me out to become an ambassador for marriage and family around the world. It never dawned on me, or the leaders of that church, that marriage ministry was something that could be done inside the local church. We all had the "it's not what is supposed to be done here; we have another agenda" mind-set.

The church must raise the banner of Hebrews 13:4, which says, "Marriage should be honored by all." Whether you are single, divorced, a single parent raising kids, or you're just here intentionally pushing or delaying marriage, you are called to honor marriage. Instead of picketing on the courthouse steps and telling the government what marriage should be, maybe the church should wake up and bring marriage back into the church. We should proclaim that we esteem marriage as highly valuable. A lot of pastors shy away from talking about marriage because of brokenness surrounding it. So many hearts have been hurt by painful marriages, divorce, and confusion about God's design for marriage between men and women. This is no excuse for passively leaving our marriages to society's whims. This has been on Satan's turf long enough. Let's bring it back to the church.

I am so proud of my two boys, Greg and Michael. They have served in parachurch marriage ministry for their entire adult lives. Both of them, along with Ted, are now working together to wake churches up to the need for healthy marriages in the church. We can turn the tide, and we ought to start in the church.

Revolutionary Idea #2—Marriage is not for everyone, but everyone must be for marriage. (See 1 Corinthians 7; Hebrews 13:4.)

First Corinthians 7 says that marriage isn't for everyone, but Hebrews 13:4 says everyone must be for marriage. The church cannot shy away from strong teaching and programming on marriage because of the hurt and pain. That is the reason we need to hit it even harder. In our church, we commit the first Sunday of every month to marriage. Our children, teens, and adults are all learning how to honor marriage together. While launching this vision, we received this letter:

> *Dear Pastor Ted,*
>
> *I just wanted to write you a note to let you know I will be praying for you and for all those who will be touched as you start the marriage series at our church.*
>
> *I have to admit my heart sank a little when you announced this new series as marriage is a very, very tough subject for me, but God once again reminded me that it is not all about me. The importance of marriage goes without saying. I look forward to you sharing how we all can go about strengthening and supporting [it].*
>
> *I am twice divorced. The first time I thought it was the right thing to do. The second divorce was not what I wanted at all. I have also watched as two of my children have gone through their own divorces.*
>
> *The guilt, the hurt, the pain that comes with*

divorce is awful. There are no winners with divorce
from the individuals directly involved to all of society.
How it must break God's heart.

If someone was about to step off the sidewalk into
the path of a speeding car, we would pray that someone
would be there to pull them to safety. This is how I feel
about divorce. Divorce is that speeding car, heading
right for that couple contemplating it. We have to
pray that that couple will be pulled to safety and out
of its path.

Thank you for all you do and may God bless you.

What a fantastic word picture and validation for why
we must teach kids, singles, and young adults to honor
marriage.

Revolutionary Idea #3—Couples will ignite around adventure. (See Ecclesiastes 9:9.)

I have a dear friend in Phoenix, Arizona, who focuses his phi-
lanthropy in the world of marriage and family ministry. In
2007, he gathered a large group of individuals in Scottsdale,
Arizona, because of their deep concern about one looming
problem: "Marriages in the local church are failing at or near
the same rate as those outside the church."

Essentially they were a potpourri group represent-
ing Texas, Tennessee, Maryland, Connecticut, California,
Missouri, Georgia, and Arizona. The group was equally

split between men and women, all married, ranging in age from twenty-one to fifty. The gathering included two senior pastors, two corporate executives, two marketing executives, a seminary student, a film company CEO, a CPA, a counselor, two stay-at-home moms, a youth pastor, two nonprofit executive directors, two marriage authors, a flight attendant, a philanthropist, a project manager, and two newlyweds.

This group was asked three questions to turn their hearts toward a whole new ministry within the local church . . .

When someone says "marriage ministry," you think . . .
The top five answers:
1. Outdated and "preachy"
2. Boring
3. Counseling and homework
4. Feminine focused
5. Once a year, parachurch based or led by someone my grandparent's age

Where would you rate your marriage on a scale of 1 to 10 (10 being the best)?*
The top three answers:
1. 5
2. 7
3. 6

*interesting to note, only one 8 and two 9s—no 10s

For a marriage ministry to work in the local church, it would have to be . . . ?

The top five answers:

1. Fun and adventure based
2. Relevant, real, and undomesticated
3. In the church, by the church, and from the pulpit
4. Peer to peer and sustainable
5. Focused on marriages going from a 5 to 10 and not marriages already at a 1 to 2

The initial group who discussed these three questions spawned countless follow-up meetings and multiple research assignments. Our goal moving forward was simple: verify or dismiss the answers given by our original group—was there something more that we were missing? Eighteen months and cross-country dialogue with counselors, couples, and pastors unfortunately surfaced the same answers. The church needed to be the catalyst of this marriage movement, and the program needed to be "peer to peer," not expert driven. Words like *fun, adventure, play,* and *laughing* became part of every meeting, and phrases like "do, live, and create" with others became the action.

In the end, research doesn't get you anything but a full file folder. We had too much information not to do something more with it, and now we just had to "reinvent marriage ministry in the local church." Simple, huh? So we began the task of finding two churches with two senior pastors who were willing to turn their churches and their own marriages inside out.

Small groups would be turned upside down and challenged to "get off the couch" and incorporate adventure/fun with couples who shared similar affinities. Small groups would not be zip-code based or focused on videos or studies, but would be built around community and creativity to "dream big, gear up, and live the adventure" with other couples. Simply put, these two pastors decided that what is currently being done in the typical local church isn't leading couples to experience a thriving marriage, and because the church's divorce rate continues to be just as high as the world's, they've pushed their "ships" toward new horizons where they can lead and discover "new oceans" together.

Revolutionary Idea #4—Couples will ignite couples. (See Proverbs 27:17; Ecclesiastes 4:12.)

When I say "marriage ministry," most pastors and churchgoers would immediately think about weekend retreats, seminars, and products provided by guys like me. The truth is, you learn more from the people you hang around. You learned how to treat the opposite sex by watching your mom and dad early on, and now your peers are your primary influence.

It's not about having the professional or the PhD instructing us and telling us what makes a marriage great. We need the Alcoholics Anonymous model, which says, if you've been sober for one month you can help somebody who has been sober for a week. We are encouraging couples to ignite other couples through adventure. If you've been married for three months, you can gain a lot from the person who has been married fifty years. But here's what I really love: The couple married fifty years can also learn a lot from the hot, passionate, on-fire newlywed couple.

Revolutionary Idea #5—For one year, the church commits one Sunday a month to marriage.

Here is where I am really proud of Ted. As a church we can be in a study series on Ephesians, or walking through the Gospels, and he pauses for one Sunday every month to blow the bugle for marriage. When you walk in our church, the banners are flying and the videos are playing. Everything is pointing toward marriage.

Here is a brief rundown of what we call igniters. There are twelve. In one calendar year, we will cover twelve key topics that are critical to every marriage.

TwoPlay . . . in the thick of the grind. When did marriage and adulthood become boring and dull? What sounds like fun to you? Refuse to allow duty and responsibility to trump fun. Ignite your inner kid, and play again.

TwoLaugh . . . at myself and lighten up. When did we get so serious? Stop with the long faces. Ignite your sense of humor.

TwoFight . . . as teammates. When did we start playing against each other? What does being on the same team look like? Let's put on the same jersey. Ignite the fight by taking up arms together.

TwoHunt . . . for the treasure behind the words. When did we stop going beneath the surface in our conversations? How can we get below the surface? Ignite your conversations by asking great questions.

TwoRisk . . . my insecurities by getting real with myself, my mate, and God. What would taking bold risks for our faith look like? Ignite your relationship with God.

TwoSweat . . . for health and wellness. When did we let ourselves go? Ignite your bodies to a healthier lifestyle. Healthy bodies make for better adventures.

TwoDrink . . . to great sex. Is our sex life dehydrated? Do we want to settle for sips or do we want to be intoxicated? Ignite the passion in the bedroom, kitchen, or even the great outdoors.

TwoLink . . . with family and friends. What can we do to better build into our friends and extended family? Do we have balanced relationships with those outside our immediate family? Ignite your relationships with other couples.

TwoFuel . . . your dreams with resources. Are we budgeted for success in marriage? Are we paving our own path, or are we keeping up with the Joneses? Ignite your finances to help fuel a more adventurous marriage.

TwoGuard . . . your marriage from a kid-centered home. Are we gifting our children with a great marriage? Ignite your home with a mom and dad who are crazy in love.

TwoBreak . . . from home. Have we left home physically, relationally, and emotionally? What cords still need cutting? Ignite your marriage by waving good-bye.

TwoFinish . . . well. What are all the reasons why we will never divorce? Ignite your commitment with a promise till death or the Lord's return.

Revolutionary Idea #6—Divorce-proofing is not enough.

Marriage ministry must be about more than divorce-proofing. We planted Woodland Hills in 2002, and we made divorce-proofing every marriage one of our goals. We set out to make sure no couple divorced, but the problem was we've seen too many couples stay together and be miserable. The goal is not to stay together and be miserable; the goal is to stay together and enjoy life with each other.

Why on earth we let marriage slip away from the church, I have no idea. There have been a lot of spineless church leaders, afraid to talk about marriage because of the demographics of their church. Then they whine and complain when the government sets out to redefine it. Shame on us. We've gone silent, and for that we repent.

We say marriage is a beautiful thing to be enjoyed between a husband and a wife for a lifetime. For the divorced person who is hurting right now, thinking, *I never, never knew it could be healed and good, and now it's too late and we've moved on*, they need an extra load of grace and encouragement today. We encourage single parents to get to the point where they can say, "No matter how marriage turned out for me, I have to walk through this with my kids by teaching them how to honor marriage and giving them a healthy perspective for the future."

When the church and its members work together to create couple-centered homes, transformation starts to happen, one family at a time. Here is a prayer you and your church can pray on behalf of the families in your community:

> Father, we want to be a church that's known in this community for helping marriages and families because we believe they're the basis of a healthy society. We know that strong families help guard against poverty, addictions, and individual brokenness. We know how critical a strong family is to the hearts of our young kids.
>
> We are doing battle for them so they won't grow up in a home with a mom and a dad who can't stand each other, or with parents who have split and believe the lie from the pit of hell that says they can divorce and stay friends for the kids. We pray that married couples would give the greatest gift to their kids, and that is a mom and a dad who are growing in their relationship in the Lord and in their love for each other.
>
> We don't have to choose between a life and a wife. We don't have to choose between a life and a husband. We can have both.
>
> It's in the name of Jesus that everyone agreed and said . . .

Add your voice to the GPLL message . . .

Connect with us at www.greatparentslousylovers.com and watch the video podcast for chapter 20.

Post your thoughts, comments, and stories on our Web site. Here are some questions from chapter 20 to get you started on your journey to a couple-centered home:

- How can your marriage ignite the marriages around you?

- What can you do to serve the marriages of your church?

- Do you agree that the church has put more focus on children, rather than marriage? Why or why not?

- What needs to happen to make marriage more of a priority in the local church?

- Why is commitment not enough in a marriage?

IGNITER DATE:

Each month focus together on one of the twelve key ignite topics we listed. How are you doing in each area, both individually and as a couple? Pray together and ask God's wisdom to help you do more than divorce-proof your marriage. Expect that God wants to help you maintain a marriage that reflects his love and commitment to us.

Notes

CHAPTER 7: BUILDING MARGIN
1. Jerry Jenkins, *Hedges* (Brentwood, TN: Wolgemuth & Hyatt, 1989), 125.

CHAPTER 8: FOUR SPIRITUAL JOURNEYS
1. G. Stanley Hall, *Adolescence: Its Psychology and Its Relations to Physiology, Anthropology, Sociology, Sex, Crime, Religion and Education* (New York: Appleton, 1904).

CHAPTER 11: YOUR CHILD'S SPIRITUAL JOURNEY
1. Nancy Gibbs, "The Growing Backlash Against Overparenting," *Time*, November 20, 2009, 34.
2. The National Commission on Terrorist Attacks upon the United States, *The 9/11 Commission Report*, http://www.9-11commission.gov/report/911Report.pdf.

CHAPTER 15: LAUGH MORE
1. Chuck Swindoll, *Laugh Again* (Dallas: Word, 1992), 13.

CHAPTER 18: SEX AFTER KIDS
1. Mayo Clinic staff, "Exercise: 7 Benefits of Regular Physical Activity," http://www.mayoclinic.com/health/exercise/HQ01676.

THE DNA OF RELATIONSHIPS
BY DR. GARY SMALLEY

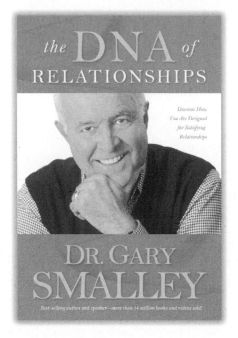

HAVE YOU EVER FELT AS IF YOU'RE . . .

Repeating the Same Mistakes in Your Relationships?

DR. GARY SMALLEY TELLS YOU
THE WHYS AND HOWS OF RELATIONSHIPS:

· Discover the fear dance that occurs in all relationships.

· Explore how to create safety in relationships.

· Cultivate healthy habits that care for your emotional needs.

· Find out how to listen to other people's emotions.

CP0166